CHRISTIAN IDENTITY AND THEOLOGICAL EDUCATION

Scholars Press

Studies in Theological Education

CHRISTIAN IDENTITY
AND
THEOLOGICAL EDUCATION

by
Joseph C. Hough, Jr.
and
John B. Cobb, Jr.

Scholars Press
Atlanta, Georgia

CHRISTIAN IDENTITY AND THEOLOGICAL EDUCATION

Joseph C. Hough, Jr.
and
John B. Cobb, Jr.

© 1985
Scholars Press

Library of Congress Cataloging in Publication Data

Hough, Joseph C.
    Christian identity and theological education.

    (Scholars Press studies in religious and theological scholarship)
    Includes bibliographical references and index.
    1. Theology—Study and teaching—United States.
2. Church. 3. Identification (Religion). I. Cobb, John B.
II. Title. III. Series.
BV4030.H68   1985   207'.73   85–10920
ISBN 0–89130–855–5 (alk. paper)

Printed in the United States of America
on acid-free paper

CONTENTS

Preface

The Association of Theological Schools, with the support of the Lilly Endowment, is engaged in a multifaceted study of theological education. This book is one result of that study. Its purpose is to make realistic proposals for revising of theological curricula appropriate to the Christian faith in the present situation. The specific proposals in Chapter V are offered as warranted by the understanding of Christian faith and church leadership presented in the earlier chapters. It is our hope that they will commend themselves for discussion and will contribute to the implementation of reforms.

The writing of this book was very much a cooperative process. Not only did the two of us work together in the actual writing of every chapter, but we also had the privilege of collaborating with our faculty colleagues in a variety of ways. Six responded to our invitation to write special papers on subjects related to the manuscript. For these papers, we are indebted to the following colleagues:

Robert J. Arnott	The Ordained Ministry and the Seminary Curriculum
David Ray Griffin	Theology and the Rise of Modern Science
Rolf Knierim	The Task of Old Testament Theology
Ronald Osborn	The Many Faces of Ministry
Dan D. Rhoades	The Internationalization of North American Theological Education?
Cornish Rogers	Black Theological Education

We are especially grateful to Ronald Osborn, whose writing formed the basis for much of our reflection in Chapter I. We also drew directly from David Griffin's paper for parts of Chapter II. But these are only the most obvious instances of our indebtedness. Every member of the faculty provided helpful comments on, and suggestions for, the manuscript. Formally, this was done at two weekend retreats in 1983 and 1984 and in ten faculty discussions, most of which focused on the papers listed above. Informally, it took place in conversations over coffee or after a long drought in committee meetings.

In some ways the process that produced the manuscript was the culmination of a continuing discussion among faculty, students, and selected congregations and pastors about the purpose of theological education. As early as 1968, we worked together to design a special education project on the role of the churches and the seminary in opposing white racism. All together, more than one hundred congregations, sixty student interns, and almost the entire faculty collaborated in that attempt to address a major issue facing the church and the world. This was followed by a similar but smaller project on the relationship of global responsibility and Christian spirituality. Thus we had more than ten years of collaboration and issue-oriented work in theological education behind us when we began our work on this book.

This does not mean that our proposals describe the existing curriculum in Claremont. They do not. Rather, they are the current proposals of two members of the faculty to our colleagues. At this point, therefore, our faculty discussions must shift from general theoretical considerations to practical and political ones.

Much of our criticism of current theological education is derived from our attempt to be sensitive to the global context of our work. We are convinced that as Christians no narrower context is allowed us. But within that context we realize that we are not addressing theological education everywhere and at all times. Instead, we are speaking primarily to those seminaries that prepare leaders for the white, middle-class, North American churches; that is, we have seminaries like our own in view. We hope that seminaries of other types can benefit from our ideas, but we want to make clear our awareness of the limitations of what we have done.

In our book we have called for a new understanding of Christian leadership, one in which practical Christian thinking goes hand in hand with reflection in practice. We hope that others will see in this book an example of the practical theology we have recommended. We have identified an issue in our own living practice. We have thought about that issue from our perspective on what it means to be Christian. And we have pointed out certain implications of the commitment to be Christian for reordering what we do in light of who we are. Throughout, we have drawn on our own experiences; that is, we have reflected as Christian theological educators on the practice of educating Christian leadership. That is practical theology as we understand it.

We are grateful to Leon Pacala of the Association of Theological Schools for including us in the Issues Research Council. Through this association we have received many helpful comments and criticisms from colleagues outside our immediate community.

We want to express our thanks to the board of the Lilly Endowment for a generous grant, without which the project would not have been possible. We are also grateful to Robert Lynn, of the Lilly Endowment, for his personal support and encouragement. Not only was he helpful in securing funding for the project, but he has also been an important conversation partner for a number of years as we have wrestled with issues in theological education. No single person has done more to generate the important current conversation about the future of theological education than he has. We are indebted to him, therefore, even beyond his support for our particular contribution to that conversation.

This book would never have been completed without the assistance of the staff at the School of Theology in Claremont. We are especially appreciative of the assistance of Marcia Doss and Sharlene Jensen. We also want to thank Ginny Becker, who applied the magic of word processing to the mix, and to Margaret Yamashita, who helped us to smooth the roughest edges of our writing.

We continue to be grateful to President Richard Cain of the School of Theology for his support and confidence. He has been generous in allowing us the time we needed to do our work, and he has been an enthusiastic participant in the project itself.

Chapter III contains material from Joseph C. Hough, Jr., "Theologian at Work," in Carl S. Dudley, ed., *Building Effective Ministry* (New York: Harper & Row, 1983). Grateful acknowledgment is made to Carl S. Dudley and Harper & Row for permission to use this material.

Claremont, August 1984

Chapter I

The Problematic of Theological Education

Anyone associated with theological education for ministers in the "main-line" Protestant churches of the United States is surely aware that there is widespread discontent with the schools providing this education. Criticisms range from charges that the curricula of the schools are too academic and have little relevance for the actual practice of the ministry, to charges that the efforts to meet this criticism have led the schools to a trivialization of their curricula. Basically, this latter criticism is an allegation that many seminaries are little more than technical schools specializing in skills training for specific organizational tasks in the institutional church. Thus, would-be reformers propose contradictory directions of change. This adds to confusion in the seminary, as beleaguered faculties, themselves often critical of their curricula and more often bewildered by the multiple demands and expectations placed upon them from a variety of sources, ponder the most recent proposals for reform.[1]

1. Farley's Theologia

A major interpretation of this confusion appears in Edward Farley's *Theologia*, which has served as the basis for the most recent round of regional discussions among representatives of seminaries in the Association of Theological Schools.[2] Farley suggests that most current proposals for reform are merely cosmetic, because they deal only with what he calls the "symptomology" of the problem of theological education. The real need is conceptual, namely, to conceive the theological unity of all theological studies. Farley argues that the loss of unity has been due, first, to the transformation of the study of theology into the study of discrete theological sciences and second, to the growing perception of the ministry as task-oriented with respect to specific functions. The consequence of these combined developments is that theological schools have expanded their curricula to accommodate the rise of the discrete sciences of theology, on the one hand, and the functional skills required by expanding organizational demands on church leadership, on the

---

[1] Joseph C. Hough, Jr., "The Politics of Theological Education," *Occasional Papers*, September 7, 1981 (Nashville: United Methodist Board of Higher Education and Ministry).
[2] Edward Farley, *Theologia* (Philadelphia: Fortress Press, 1983).

other. The uneasy coexistence of these two types of subject matter consti-
titute what Farley describes as the "professional" model of theological
education, with its sharp theory-versus-practice distinction. Needless to
say, that professional model lacks unity and coherence.

How, then, can the unity and coherence of theological studies be
restored? Farley's answer to that question is complex, but the crux of his
argument appears in his comments on Schleiermacher's proposals in his
Brief Outline.[3] Schleiermacher's task was to justify inclusion of theology
in the new university. In Berlin, von Humboldt had projected the idea of
the university as a congeries of specialists, each of whom focused
research in a "discipline," with a distinct methodology and with field
coherence.[4] Theology was under pressure to demonstrate that it was such
a discipline despite the criticism that its dogmatic or ecclesiastical character prevented it from being such a positive science.[5]

Schleiermacher argued that theological studies were united by reference to one of the three major professions, that is, the ministry. Like
medical studies and legal studies, there were various aspects of theological studies, especially the historical disciplines, that had a distinct methodology and that yielded verifiable, positive knowledge. But also like law
and medicine, theology as a whole was unified by its concern for matters
affecting the practice of a major profession.[6] In other words, the unity of
theological studies lay in the fact that all parts of its subject matter were
determined by their relevance to the needs of the church for leadership.
Farley labels this unifying model "the clerical paradigm," or the "teleological" understanding of the unity of theological studies.[7]

Farley also sees in Schleiermacher's book a "deeper" understanding
of the unity of theological studies. At its base, the unity of theological
studies is the "essence of Christianity . . . manifest in its reality and
truth."[8] Farley quite candidly and correctly states that Schleiermacher
never makes this criterion explicit, but he argues that it is implied. Farley attributes our current confusion to the growing dominance of
Schleiermacher's clerical paradigm and the eventual loss of Schleiermacher's material conception of the unity of theological studies. Any
attempt at reform that confines itself to tampering with the clerical

[3] Ibid., pp. 93–98.

[4] Burton P. Bledstein, *The Culture of Professionalism* (New York: Norton, 1976),
pp. 312–17, 327–28.

[5] Gerhard Ebeling, *The Study of Theology*, trans. Duane Priebe (Philadelphia: Fortress
Press, 1978), p. 85.

[6] Farley, op. cit., pp. 85–87. Cf. also Hough, op. cit., p. 1; Friedrich Schleiermacher,
Brief Outline of the Study of Theology, trans. William Farrar (Edinburgh: T. & T.
Clark, 1850, American Library edition, 1963), pp. 91–97.

[7] Farley, op. cit., pp. 87–88.

[8] Ibid., pp. 93–94.

paradigm is, in Farley's view, doomed to failure. Only a recovery of the material basis for unity, in Farley's words, *theologia* itself, can lead to genuine reform in theological education.

The latter half of Farley's book, then, is given to the pursuit of some methodological procedures for recovering the material basis for the unity of theological studies. But the material basis itself, *theologia*, remains maddeningly elusive. At one point, *theologia* is described as ". . . a sapiential knowledge engendered by grace and divine self-disclosure."[9] In other places, Farley states that it is the "knowledge which attends faith in its concrete existence," but it is "not identical with piety."[10] Again, *theologia* is the "knowledge of the mythos and tradition of the world of faith, the ascertaining of its truth, and the incorporation of both into the contemporary situation." It is ". . . an activity, a life process."[11] Thus, if we understand Farley, all of this might mean that *theologia* is reflective understanding, shared by members of a Christian community regarding who they are and what they are do to, given their concrete world-historical situation.

If this is an accurate reading of what Farley means by "material unity," then we agree that *theologia* is essential for recovering the unity of theological education. But (a) we are not satisfied with Farley's account of *theologia*, and (b) we disagree with his view that the "clerical paradigm" is the problem.

(a) Farley's account of *theologia* is unsatisfactory in two ways. First, it is too abstract and formal to provide guidance for theological education. Indeed, it may be more accurate to say that Farley's book is a call for *theologia* and a reflection on the methodology by which theologians might eventually attain it. But it does not offer the *theologia* needed as a basis for reform.

In this respect Farley's book is all too typical of contemporary theological work. Much of it has retreated from addressing the urgent issues of faith to reflection about the methodology by which such engagement should be accomplished. This move is motivated by the desire to achieve greater reliability and, therefore, greater consensus. But in fact, disputes about method are as divisive as are those about doctrine, and the selection of a method is at least as much affected by theological convictions as the latter are shaped by methods.

A theological faculty seeking to act out the implications of Farley's book might devote its efforts to understanding and adopting his theological method as the basis for a curriculum. This would be far different from basing a curriculum on *theologia*. It would accentuate the gulf

---

9 Ibid., p. 153.
10 Ibid., p. 160.
11 Ibid., p. 164.

between the content of theological education and the practice of ministry, substituting an academic concern about a particular way of
approaching the understanding of faith for the faith itself.

What is needed today as a basis for reforming theological education
is a strong conviction about who we are as a Christian people. It is true
that no such assertions will command universal assent. Indeed, a quest
for total agreement is a hopeless one. The hope instead is that the discussion precipitated by concrete proposals will lead to conclusions that will
motivate action. This is not impossible.

Our first objection to Farley's treatment of *theologia* is that it is too
abstract and indirect. Our second concern is that even if it were fleshed
out, it might be inadequate and even misleading. In our view, the global
crisis in which we live must be the context of Christian understanding
today. This means also that every doctrine is closely connected to practice. It is immensely important that *theologia* be accurate and clear, but
it is not the right *theologia* for the Christian community unless it is in
the service of God's work in and for the world. We are convinced that
this work is concretely historical and that *theologia* must draw believers
into the service of the indivisible salvation of people and societies suffering from hunger, oppression, and despair as a result of the demonic
political, economic, and social forces now at work. This certainly does
not exclude from the province of God's action an interior, existential
change in individuals or the empowerment and guidance of the church.
But we fear that Farley's *theologia* would so focus on personal and
ecclesial life as to distract attention from the historical horizons of the
world God loves.

(b) Although we agree with Farley as to the importance of *theologia*
as the basis for unity of theological education, we do not see that as
minimizing the need for a "teleological" unity. As Schleiermacher saw,
that unity is constituted by the aim to help educate professional leaders
for the church. Because historically most such leaders have been clergy,
this has been called the "clerical paradigm," and Farley judges that the
growing dominance of the clerical paradigm is the source of much of
our confusion in theological education.

If by "theological education" is meant the education of all Christians
in the faith, then the dominance of a clerical paradigm would be cata-
strophic. Theological education in this basic sense is the right and need
of every Christian. It is the responsibility of the entire church. This education has its basis and unity in *theologia*. If this were Farley's meaning,
we would fully agree with him.

But within the context of this encompassing theological education,
the church has chosen over many centuries to establish separate institutions to further the preparation of church leaders. It is fitting that the
education in these schools be directed toward this goal and that this

direction give to the curriculum its unity. *Theologia* is the basis of unity of *all* theological education. Apart from *theologia* there would be no church needing leaders. Leaders require an especially full and reliable understanding of *theologia*; so this is essential to their special education as well as to what they share with all Christians. But the unity of their special education, whether or not it includes anything other than *theologia*, will be teleological, that is, it will be guided by the aim of providing the special education appropriate to church leaders.

This has been true since the rise of medieval universities in which theology, medicine, and law were seen as the great professions. Theology then was studied by those who wished to serve the church. To be sure, it was the study of divine things that they pursued, but their concentrated study was exceptional, not characteristic of all Christians. Moreover, the completion of their studies almost always was followed by an appointment to some leadership post in the service of the church. Their knowledge was specialized, and it was assumed that their "vocation" was to be in the service of the church. The current problem for the theological school is *not* that it is a "professional" school, dominated by the "clerical paradigm." Rather it is that the church has become uncertain and confused as to what consitutes appropriate professionalism. There can be no clear unity to theological education until there is recovery of clarity about the nature of professional leadership within the church.

2. Ministerial "Characters"

What is the "professional minister"? Ronald Osborn, in a perceptive, historical study, has pointed out that in certain periods of American history, there have emerged dominant ministerial types who defined the profession for that time. These types were not created simply by the expectations of persons in the churches. On the contrary, the expectations in the churches were so widely shared that ministerial characters became genuine social leadership characters.[12] These characters arose in relation to certain theological concepts of the church and ministry resident in the Christian tradition, as those concepts were influenced by the

---

[12] The term *social character* is drawn from Alisdair McIntyre's *After Virtue* (Notre Dame, IN: University of Notre Dame Press, 1981). McIntyre develops his notion of characters by referring to Japanese noh plays and English morality plays. He suggests that in these plays, there are certain stock characters that are so representative as to be immediately recognizable by the audience. Therefore, if one recognizes these "characters," one can also readily interpret the intentions of the actors who play them. They are also central to the plot, and other actors always play their roles in relation to these central characters. Drawing an analogy from these characters, McIntyre argues that in any culture there are certain key dominant *social characters* who define the culture in some ways. For example, the distinctive characters of Victorian English culture were the Public School Headmaster, the Explorer, and the Engineer (cf. pp. 26ff.).

churches' peculiar socio-historical locations. A particular character arose and became embedded in the minds of church people and widely recognized both within and outside of the church. The character then receded in importance, as both theological and socio-cultural movements interacted to give birth to a new "character."[13]

Serious problems arose for the concept of ministry during those times when the theological bases for a particular image were radically challenged by intellectual criticism within and outside the church, or when broad social changes imposed new demands on the minister as a leader of an institution. Usually, both social changes and criticism combined to create confusion about the ministry. When the criticism was intense and change rapid, the confusion became overwhelming. This was because the memory of the old characters remained powerful in church lore long after the new characters had effectively displaced them in the institutional life of the churches and even in the perception of the society at large. In such times of crisis, the society's instutional expectations of the minister are in serious tension with the passing ministerial character. This tension, then, remains until a new character has emerged from the coalescing expectations to replace the old one. This social situation literally leaves ministers on their own without any defining character.

There were a variety of characters in the early years of the church's life in the United States, and each was important to defining ministry. However, the Master was the dominant character during the seventeenth and eighteenth centuries, particularly in the Reformed churches. And it was the development of the ministry in the mold of this character that dominated the efforts of theological educators through the nineteenth century.

Who was the Master? Essentially, he was the authoritative teacher whose roots are in the history of the sages of the orient and the rabbis of ancient Judaism. In Calvin's Geneva, the ideal of the authoritative teacher was institutionalized, and in Puritan New England, the Master strode across the landscape with daring based on learning and grounded in popular esteem and affection. He had something to say, and the people listened as he spoke about the authoritative teaching given to his care. The Master's authority rested on an existing authoritative body of literature and a personal knowledge of that literature. He was the one who was authorized in some way to teach it. This character is present and dominant whenever the focus of religious expectations, beliefs, and aspirations in the Christian community allows for, and even affirms, the existence of a body of knowledge necessary for the salvation of the

[13] Ronald Osborn, "The Many Faces of Ministry" (unpublished manuscript, Claremont, 1982), p. 15. See also the discussion of early ministerial types in Thomas F. Omeara, *Theology of Ministry* (New York: Paulist Press, 1983), pp. 95ff.

world, and also the right and duty of people to be instructed by one who has mastered that knowledge and is authorized to teach it.[14]

When the Master was the dominant character, it was generally assumed that preparation for ministry required study in the university. Until the rise of the modern university, divinity education consisted simply of study in the university, crowned by the study of the things of God. The Master, therefore, was a learned person, one who spoke with authority in general. He was expected to give intellectual leadership in the traditional scholarly disciplines, and in addition, he increasingly spoke with clarity and authority on issues of public policy.[15]

At this time, ministerial "formation" was closely related to university education. Holiness or piety was not achieved by ordinary "enthusiasms"; in fact, such enthusiasms were looked upon with suspicion. Rather holiness was achieved by the study of texts. The study of ancient languages, scripture, history, philosophy, logic, and so on, all were, therefore, for the sake of understanding authoritative texts, and piety was identical with the understanding of and love for those texts. Therefore, the Master was at once learned and pious. He was "formed" as a ministerial character by his learning.[16]

In summary, the very idea of the ministerial character, the Master, carried with it the expectation that, in general, the fundamental preparation for the ministry was a classical education, which, of course, included the study of scripture and divine things. What ministers learned in their educational experience cohered nicely with the beliefs and expectations that converged to give credence to the Master as a social character. As long as the Master remained the dominant social character, then, the only problem for theological education was that university education be done well—that the minister's education be the best classical education that could be offered.

During the nineteenth century many leaders in theological education in the United States came under the influence of scholars from the Continent, particularly those in Germany. Several of them studied in Germany and there became acquainted with the study of the theological curriculum itself. German faculties introduced students to the curriculum consisting of courses designed to outline the various independent disciplines in the curriculum, each with a particular methodology and literature. Moreover, some rationale was usually provided for both the presence of each of the disciplines and also a theory about their interrelatedness or unity. In fact, there developed a literature on the theory of theological education which

---

[14] Ibid., Chap. 3, pp. 42–43.
[15] Ibid., Chap. 2, p. 51.
[16] Ibid., Chap. 2, p. 43; see also Farley, op. cit., pp. 7ff.

came to be known as theological encyclopedia.[17] The standard pattern of these encyclopedias consisted of sacred literature, dogmatics, ecclesiastical history, and practical theology, what Farley has labeled the "fourfold pattern."

American leaders brought back to the United States their fascination with theological encyclopedia and set about to change the face of theological education in the United States. By the end of the nineteenth century, then, the fourfold pattern had become normative for the theological curriculum. There were, of course, wide variations among the seminaries, but generally it was assumed that the study of theology was necessary for ministers and that such study included the mastery of the literature of certain defined specialized "sciences" of theology.

For our purposes, it is important to remember that the answer to the question about the nature of education for the ministry was derived in this case from the specifications of those fields or sciences of theology that were intrinsic to the subject matter itself. In other words, education for the ministry was instruction in the most authoritative literature of the field of theology as a whole, and what was authoritative was defined by the specialists in the sub-disciplines or sciences, which, taken together, formed the study of theology. The authority of these fields rested on their status as sciences in the eyes of the university.

The dominance of the fourfold pattern for theological study was largely the work of theological scholars and teachers. They built the momentum that led to the adoption of the fourfold pattern as normative for the education of ministers. It was an adaptation to the new understanding of the university rather than to changes in the ministerial character. This fourfold pattern was simply an attempt to find a new expression of the educational requirements necessary to ensure the authority of the Master. It was a move to shift the legitimation of ministerial authority from dogma to the methodology and literature of the scientific study of religion. Thus, the Master retained social power long after there were certain clear signs of his demise. In theological schools, this image of the professional minister still remains as a dominant force. Faculties continue to urge the model of the "learned minister" as normative. What has changed, as Farley has so ably demonstrated, was the content of what consitututed learning. It changed from a general knowledge of humanistic learning crowned by the study of divine things, to specialized study of religion in discreet, and sometimes disconnected, disciplines, some of which were only remotely related to the work of the minister.

---

[17] Robert W. Lynn, "Notes Toward a History: Theological Encyclopedia and the Evolution of American Seminary Curriculum, 1808–1968" (unpublished manuscript, read at Vanderbilt University in fall 1979), pp. 15–17. For an extensive treatment of theological encyclopedia, see Farley, op. cit., Chaps. 3, 4.

3. *The Decline of the Master Character*

Despite the best efforts of theological schools to maintain the image of professional ministers as authoritative teachers, the actual social character changed. This has been the result of a number of factors, of which we shall trace two here. (a) The actual situation of the church in the United States has demanded different types of leadership, and (b) the modern understanding of the profession has undercut the Master as the dominant social character of the minister.

(a) On the political front, the new nation soon wrote into its foundational political documents the principles of freedom of religion and separation of church and state, which meant that the minister more and more functioned in the climate of religious pluralism. Soon, a variety of "authoritative traditions" were in open competition with each other in an increasingly free marketplace of religious ideas.

The organizational character of the churches changed significantly as a result. They were transformed from parish-oriented organizations, with some social authority, to voluntary organizations. Membership in these organizations was based on the consent of the individual believer. The authority of the religious leaders was correspondingly based not on their ability to interpret a body of authoritative teaching, but on their ability to persuade religiously inclined persons of the importance, if not the superiority, of their own teaching. This signaled, Osborn notes, that the Master was being replaced by the *Revivalist* and the *Pulpiteer*. These were two new characters who, by the end of the nineteenth century, dominated popular perceptions of the religious actors on the social stage. Oratory replaced instruction as the dominant mode of clergy activity, and there arose a group of widely acclaimed "princes of the pulpit." Their success established a virtual identification in the American mind of the minister with preaching, and this development was augmented by the success of the Revivalist, for whom, also, preaching was the primary activity. Although the revivalists concentrated all of their energies on the conversion of sinners, and the sinners were outside the church (in theory), they nonetheless shaped the assumptions of the churches, and increasingly, the expectations of the surrounding culture. Although revivalism began on the frontier, it subsequently moved into the Eastern cities and, by the end of the nineteenth century, the whole style of American preaching, even in the established churches, has been affected.[18]

Most of the ministers in the United States during the nineteenth century did not possess the oratorical skills of the Pulpiteer or the Revivalist. Rather they quietly undertook the task of establishing churches as the

---

[18] Osborn, op. cit., Chap. 2, pp. 19ff.

nation expanded. It was these ordinary persons who founded new congregations, built church buildings, organized the institutional life of the churches into regional groupings, and set about educating the masses of persons who were swept into church membership.

> In the space of a hundred years, they transformed the religious situation in America. Where the churches had gathered into the fold only about one person in twenty when the young nation began, these work-a-day ministers brought in, instructed, motivated, organized and equipped such numbers of people, that by 1890, church membership made up virtually 40% of the vastly expanded population.[19]

In the midst of all this building and activity, the minister as Master was finally overwhelmed. Even though influential Pulpiteers and Revivalists still developed personal authority and could even be heard as authoritative leaders in the society at large on occasion, the new dominant ministerial character was formed by the hordes of ministers who assumed organizational leadership in countless churches and church organizations. Thus, by the turn of the century, the image of the minister was not primarily the Pulpiteer, and the Master played only to the theater of theological faculties. It was instead the *Builder*, the organizer and motivator of organizations who emerged as the dominant ministerial character.

(b) During the period in which political and social factors changed the ministerial role and social character, a new world view changed the understanding of the professional. The cornerstone of this world view was a new scientific understanding of the universe as a mechanical system that operated according to fixed laws. Rational humans, by observation of the actual phenomena of nature, could understand how the universe operated. Because the universe was "lawful," it was possible to construct an empirically-based scientific theory. Such a scientific theory could then be tested by further observation and confirmed or modified on the basis of the empirical evidence gained by that observation.

If the working of nature could be understood in this way, observers who understood the causes might well intervene in the process, and use their understanding to manipulate it. In this way they could mitigate human suffering; and hence scientific theory was seen to have tremendous potential for improving the human situation if that theory were

---

[19] Ibid., Chap. 3, p. 45. In the midst of all this building, racial segregation and discrimination continued. In the postwar and Reconstruction period, those problems were even exacerbated in many parts of the country. With the vast urban migration of blacks during the 1950s and 1960s, those problems were transferred to the cities. What remains today is a curious anomaly—a church that claims to be Christian that still has within its own life the problem of racism and all the exclusivism that that entails. We shall have more to say about this in subsequent chapters, as it is part of the reality of our present historical situation.

properly applied. It could be used to develop scientifically-based techniques that could ensure progress and prosperity for humanity for the foreseeable future.

Thus was born what Donald Schoen has called the "Technological Program . . . the idea that human progress would be achieved by harnessing science to create technology for the achievement of human ends."[20] Though spawned by the emergence of the natural sciences, this technological program was not long confined to the natural sciences. Eighteenth century philosophers, impressed by the stunning discoveries of natural science, envisioned a similar methodology being applied to all human knowledge. This meant not only that the natural world could be understood by the application of the scientific method but also that the laws of human social behavior could be formulated on the basis of empirical observation. Theories of human action derived from thoroughly scientific observations, then, might become the basis for a technology of humanity and society, which could yield progress in political, social, and moral affairs similar to that already being achieved in the understanding and control of nature. In sum, society, like nature, was subjected to the technological program. Empirically-based theory could be applied rationally so as to open the possibility of a concrete, this-worldly "heavenly city" for humanity, created by the application of scientific theory to human affairs, social, political and moral.[21]

It was in this milieu, late in the nineteenth century, that the modern idea of "profession" came into view. We have already noted that the three traditional professions were divinity, law, and medicine. All three were impacted significantly, but the new understanding of the profession opened the door to many additional social roles. Any social role that involved the application of theory to resolve recognized problems could now be a profession. All that was required was that the theory and the problem be clarified in their relative autonomy and that a system be devised for recognizing those who are responsibly equipped to serve society as professionals in relation to a particular problem set.

The first of the new professions was engineering. Utilizing the discoveries of physics and chemistry, engineers achieved impressive results in the design of machines and industrial infrastructures. But of the traditional professions, it was, above all, medicine that was best able to adapt itself to the new model; and practice-oriented researchers made important progress on both the diagnosis and treatment of human disease.

---

[20] Donald Schoen, *The Reflective Practioner* (New York: Basic Books, 1983), p. 31. In the following paragraphs, we rely on Schoen's work in developing our own statement about the modern idea of the profession.

[21] Cf. Carl L. Becker, *The Heavenly City of the 18th Century Philosophers* (New Haven, CT: Yale University Press, 1932).

In both cases, the emerging idea of the profession was an instrumental one. Because it was assumed that industrial development is a desirable human end, it was appropriate for engineering to devise the means whereby new knowledge in the physical sciences could be deployed to advance industrial development. Because of this, the profession of engineering came into prominence alongside the Industrial Revolution. Or again, since human health was a desirable goal, it was appropriate for the medical profession to devise techniques whereby the new scientific knowledge could be deployed in order to progress toward disease control and to advance human physical well-being generally.[22]

If engineering and medicine are prototypical professions, then certain characteristics of any profession as it has been viewed in the modern period can be generalized from them.

First, a profession is based on a body of scientific knowledge which is accumulated by objective empirical observation and verified by experimentation. That body of knowledge is subjected to a pattern of interpretation and organized into hypothetical models. As such, it becomes a theoretical base for the practice of the profession.

Second, the professional as a practitioner applies this research-based theory to a set of problems. It is assumed that the problem-set to be solved is important in order to achieve certain ends desired by a pool of clients. Professional practice, then, was problem-solving; and expertise in problem-solving for a specific pool of clients interested in a certain problem-set was what defined a particular profession.

Third, it is assumed that expertise in problem-solving is generalizable, so that a certain "theory of practice" will evolve. The techniques of the professionals themselves, which have enabled them over time to be successful through trial and error, finally develop into a pattern of tried and true technical methods of problem-solving. In other words, the modern professional devises a technology of the profession that can be taught to future practitioners so that they may be certified as possessing the same problem-solving skills.

Professionals, then, were not basic researchers, nor were they innovators. They were those who employed the knowledge gained in basic research for solving problems in accordance with a developed technology focused on a well-defined problem-set. Professional education in the United States also was profoundly affected by this modern idea of the professional.

The new understanding of what it means to be a professional had its effect on the self-understanding of ministers. But its implications were resisted by theological educators. The conflict was not between the church and the university. Theological educators had already adopted the model

---

[22] See Schoen, op. cit., Chap. 2; see also Bledstein, op. cit., pp. 121ff.

of theological education developed in the German university. Rather they were opposing a new university model based on a different understanding of professions. The problem was that the new model was more appropriate, at least superficially, to the dominant ministerial character of Builder. Unwilling to surrender the ideal of the Master, adapted to the German view that what is mastered are academic disciplines, seminary faculties were nonetheless compelled to make ad hoc concessions to the new professional model. The result was the confusion we have noted.

4. *Theological Education for Builders*

Recognizing the incongruity between the fourfold pattern and the actual social character of the minstry, William Rainey Harper in 1899 proposed a thoroughgoing reform of theological education along the lines required by the new understanding of professions.[23] Harper sensed that a major change had occurred in the social character of the ministry, and he was quite adamant in his insistence that theological schools should recognize that change by making sweeping reforms, which would enable ministerial education to correspond to the reigning ministerial character. He was convinced that the university as a whole was not simply the repository of ancient traditions. In accord with the modern understanding of the professions, it should be the locus for training of a dynamic leadership, which would enable the nation to meet the challenges of the rapid changes accompanying the growth and expansion of industry and the developing complexity of both political and social organizations. Harper was insistent, therefore, that the proper role for the university was to be the locus of practical training for all the professions, including ministry. His suggested reforms of theological education were aimed at providing the kind of education that would prepare ministers to function effectively in a variety of the new organizational roles being created by the Builders. In other words, the seminary was to reorganize itself to prepare the Builders to do their building well. Learning was still to be important, but what constituted learning was the mastery of techniques that would increase the effectiveness of leadership.

The study of the Bible, church history, and theology were too entrenched for Harper's model to command a wide following. But the new understanding of professions nevertheless had a pervasive effect on the thinking of theological educators. It was widely felt that ministerial practice should have a base in theory. Harper had recognized that this would relate it to the social sciences, and he thus advocated including them in the curriculum. Theological educators, unwilling to follow him

---

[23] William Rainey Harper, "Shall the Theological Curriculum Be Modified and How?" *American Journal of Theology*, 1899, pp. 45–46. We are grateful to Robert Lynn for calling this article to our attention.

in the depreciation of history and theology, had two options. First, they could claim that the proper theory base for ministerial practice was to be found in the biblical, historical, and theological disciplines. Second, they could acknowledge the need for the social sciences and allow them a limited role, either as separate disciplines, or in conjunction with their application. Both procedures have been followed, but neither has worked well. Efforts to display the classical theological disciplines as the theory base for practice have met with limited success, but the social sciences have been accorded too little space to function effectively as an alternative base.

Students' complaints about the curricula being too "academic" and not "practical" enough reflected the fact that the research and teaching in the subspecialties of scientific theology had never been designed to be a theory base for the problem-set of the ministry. Instead they were designed to produce a theory base for teaching specialists in the university faculties in religious studies. Student criticisms, then, were not merely manifestations of what Bernard Barber has described as the normal "structural strain" between theoreticians of the university professional school and practioners in the field.[24] That recognizable phenomenon of any professional school has been compounded in the seminaries by the fact that the primary "theory" being taught is not capable of serving as an expanding and critical base for ministerial practice.

So much for the "theory" of the theological curriculum. What about the practice? We have indicated that the dominant understanding of ministerial practice changed significantly during the nineteenth century. The Master gave away to the Pulpiteer and then to the Builder. But the Builder is a character who requires some agreement on the purpose of building. Without a clear purpose, the Builder cannot function well. This ministerial character, the product of an age confident in its dreams and destiny, faded in the thirties and forties as the church's mission became less clear. Along with the other older characters of ministry, it has residual powers, but the social conditions for the dominance of the eighteenth, nineteenth and early twentieth century models no longer exist.

5. The Pastoral Director

Recognizing this to be the case, H. Richard Niebuhr wrote at mid-century that there really was no single model of ministry which was clearly dominant in the church or in the society at large. What he suggested, then, was the outline of an emerging understanding of the

---

[24] Bernard Barber, "A Sociology of the Professions," *Daedalus*, Fall 1963, p. 676; see also E. C. Hughes, "Professions," *Daedalus*, Fall 1963, p. 661.

ministry—the Pastoral Director—which had many similarities to Osborn's character, the Builder.[25]

There were clear differences, however. For one thing, Builders did their building confidently, assuming that there was a general social consensus on the importance of their work and a relatively clear understanding of the purpose of the institutions they were building, whereas Niebuhr saw that the consensus had disappeared. He based his proposal for the Pastoral Director on the *hope* for a growing consensus about the purpose of the church. It was, after all, the heyday of Neo-orthodoxy in 1956, and there was general optimism about the possibilities of ecumenical theology.

Another subtle difference lay in the perception of the functions of the minister. The Builders saw themselves as charged with designing, constructing, and expanding institutions for people who had been swept into the churches by the Revivalists. The Pastoral Directors in contrast emphasized maintaining institutions already built. They were *pastoral*, concentrating on counseling of all kinds for the congregation, but they were also *directors*, those who managed the church from their offices. To be sure, the Pastoral Directors did their work in the context of edification, the upbuilding of the faith of the Christian community, but this was now done primarily in a new functional mode. The traditional functions of the preacher, the teacher, and the priest receded in importance and the management and counseling functions became more and more dominant. In this sense, Niebuhr's model was prophetic. But in another sense, it was mistaken. There did not emerge any theological consensus on the purpose of the church. Indeed, that problem is even more serious today than it was in Niebuhr's time, and the theological climate now seems less conducive to consensus building than it did then to him. Confusion about the ministry has increased. Reeling under the impact of post-Neo-orthodox theological criticism and the resulting cacophony of theological voices, and working in congregations with vastly differing expectations, it is little wonder that ministers find no authoritative basis for their profession.

6. *The Emergence of the Manager and the Therapist*

Ironically, however, it is precisely this confusion that has set the stage for the new dominant ministerial characters. When there is no clear consensus on what the Builder is to build, when it is not clear just what the Master is to teach, and when the functions of the Pastoral Director are cut loose from their theological moorings, then what can be said about the purpose of the ministry?

Generally, individual ministers are left to discern the expectations of

[25] H. Richard Niebuhr, *The Purpose of the Church and Its Ministry* (New York: Harper & Row, 1956), pp. 48ff.

their congregations. Having discovered those expectations, they must motivate participation, help the members articulate their objectives, and devise strategies by which the expressed goals of the congregation can be reached. In this way they secure continuing consent to their leadership.

Because this new mode of functioning lacks any special Christian character, it is open to being modeled on the character of leadership in other social institutions. In fact, since social context plays so great a role in determining the character of ministry at any given time, it is to be expected that without any strong consensus in the churches on the nature and purpose of ministry, the dominant leadership characters in the society in general will also appear as the dominant understanding of the leadership in the churches as well.

What, then, is the dominant leadership character of our time? According to Alisdair McIntyre, it is the *Manager*, a definite social character who embodies the modern professional paradigm. Managers are experts in managerial science. They have the knowledge of the theory of how organizations work, the technology of organizations. They do not pretend to determine organizational goals. That task is outside their professional expertise. What they offer is their effective assistance to an organization in solving its internal problems so that it may more efficiently attain its goals, whatever these may be.

What the Manager does for the organization, the *Therapist*, another social character, does for the individual. Though not as dominant socially as the Manager, the Therapist is also a significant and recognizable social character. Like Managers, Therapists do not engage in debate about goals; they deal only with means. They seek to enable individual clients to discover their own values and goals, and to devise effective means by which those values and goals may be achieved or embodied.[26]

The Manager and the Therapist—these are the dominant social leadership characters in our culture, and so it is not surprising that Osborn's intuition led him to suggest that they have become the dominant images of the ministry as well. A careful look at the portrait of confusion about the ministry that Osborn paints yields at least this consensus. Whatever else the churches in the main-line Protestant denominations may want of their ministers, they want leaders who manage well and counsel effectively.[27]

7. *The Problem for Theological Education*

What conclusions can be drawn? Theological education is torn between academic norms, defined chiefly as excellence in the historical disciplines, and modern professional norms defined in terms of excellence

---

[26] McIntyre, op. cit., pp. 26ff.

[27] Osborn, Chap. 4, pp. 15ff.; see also James Gustafson, "The Clergy in the United States," *Daedalus* 92 (4), Fall 1963, pp. 735ff.

in performing the functions church leaders are expected to perform.[28] On the one hand is the character of the Master; on the other, that of the Manager. Partly as a result of this tension, theological schools do not succeed well by either standard.

If resistance within theological faculties to the downplaying of historical disciplines were simply the self-interest of academicians or the institutional desire for prestige in the university, the church should act now vigorously to reform its professional schools along the lines that Harper suggested. But this is not the case. When Harper wrote, he could assume that the church knew its own identity and what it wanted to do. It needed leaders to help implement its evident purposes, and hence he could propose the modern professional paradigm for the preparation of ministers. But if the seminaries had followed his lead at that time, the church would be worse off now than it is. It would have lost not only its sense of shared purpose but also such access to its heritage as it has retained. As long as that heritage is kept alive, at least in theological education, church leaders will retain the possibility of an authentically Christian renewal.

Further, the church is never simply one social institution among others. Only if it were could its leadership be adequately developed by models drawn from other professional schools. Of course, the church *is* one institution among others. Most North American congregations are predominantly middle-class voluntary associations, with all the habits and expectations of other such associations. To ignore this reality and to fail to prepare ministers to deal with it would be foolish. But if it were to accept this reality as the norm, the church would cease to be the church at all. The self-understanding of even these middle-class voluntary-association churches is not separable from their identity as Christian and their commitment to Christian practice. The history of what God has done in the world is intrinsic to that self-definition. It cannot be irrelevant to the qualifications for leadership, and it will inevitably bring under judgment some of the habits and expectations of middle-class religion. This means also that the church cannot accept the dominance of the Manager and the Counselor models for its own leaders; it must acknowledge the power of these social characters, but work against them.

Although we much prefer the confusion of existing seminary curricula to the consistency of Harper's model, we are far from satisfied. We believe that as a result of the current confusion, much of the time and energy given to theological education is misdirected. Although we

---

[28] See David Schuller, Milo Brekke, and Merton Strommer, eds., *Ministry in America* (San Francisco: Harper & Row, 1980). See also Samuel Blizzard, "The Minister's Dilemma," *Christian Century*, April 25, 1956, pp. 508–10. Ministers themselves know what is expected and organize their time accordingly—even if they do so reluctantly.

rejoice in the teaching of the Bible and church history, we believe that it is too much geared to interest in disciplinary scholarship and too little to the real needs of the church. Although we are glad that the social sciences have found a place in the curriculum, we do not think they should try to function as the theory base for practice. Indeed, in general we contend that the organization of theological curricula in terms of either academic disciplines or theory and practice is pernicious.

To propose an alternative is the purpose of this book. Farley is correct that this requires the recovery of *theologia*. For us, this means the clarification of Christian identity as the basis for Christian practice. In Chapter II this identity is developed as the internal history or memory by which Christians live individually and corporately. The church is defined by its commitment to keep that memory alive and to express it in present practice. In Chapter III we spell out in eleven images of the church what *we* see as this meaning of the memory for Christians today. The concern of the seminary must be to help prepare persons who will be able to keep this memory alive and to lead the church to become more of what this memory now calls it to be.

If, as a professional school, the seminary were compelled to adopt the modern paradigm of theory and its expert application, the curricular problem would remain puzzling indeed. The historical study, apart from which Christian identity is lost, would have to be separated from the professional education of the minister. But the modern paradigm is losing credibility as a guide to professional education generally. In Chapter IV we describe a new understanding of the professional as Reflective Practioner, accept that, and subsume it in a broader image of the professional church leader as Practical Theologian. We believe that the "clerical" or "professional" paradigm can provide sufficient unity to theological education only when the professional in question is understood in this way.

There is a range of church leadership professions for which theological education is needed. Much of the need is common to all of them. Most of Chapter V discusses the curriculum appropriate to the academic preparation of all church leaders as practical Christian thinkers. However, professional church leaders share with other professionals the role of reflective practitioners. This role is specific to the practice in question. Because the dominant expectation of the seminary is that it contribute to the education of pastors, a portion of this chapter considers how it can help its students become reflective pastoral practitioners.

Finally we offer an example of a six-semester curriculum that would implement the proposals made in Chapter V. The purpose is not to suggest that this is the correct curriculum for all seminaries, or even for any one; rather, it is offered only to show that the proposals are practicable.

Chapter II
The Identity of the Church

The theological school is to be understood as a professional school. As such, its primary purpose is the education of professional leadership for the church. However, as we showed in Chapter I, there is great confusion about what constitutes a proper understanding of the professional ministry. As a result of that confusion, there is little basis for an understanding of the profession of ministry to distinguish it from the model of professionalism most clearly represented by what McIntyre has identified as the dominant social character of organizational leadership, the Manager.

We do not deny the need for managerial expertise in the profession of the ministry. Yet ministers are not the managers of just any organization; they exercise their leadership in the church. The church has a variety of organizations, but these organizations, if they are to be authentically church organizations, must be understood as expressions of the church's theological understanding of itself.

That theological understanding is what provides unity to church organizations. Effective church leadership, then, must be capable of guiding the church in developing its own theological identity so that its organizations will be authentic expressions of that identity. Church organizations will then provide a proper structural context within which and from which genuine Christian practice may be nurtured and guided in the world.

If the theological school is to be a school for professional church leadership, the understanding of what it is to be a Christian community in the world will be the aim of its research and pedagogy. And it is this theological understanding that will form the basis for its curriculum and the criterion for its practice.

1. *The Horizon of Inquiry*

How shall the theological understanding of the church be determined? One approach would be to examine official expressions by church bodies or prestigious theologians as to the nature of the church. The recent Lima accord is especially worthy of study. This approach locates the understanding of the church in the history of theology.

This approach, as well as others, is legitimate, helpful, and important. The church provides an inexhaustible object of investigation, and the better it is understood, the better its professional leadership can be educated. Meanwhile, hard decisions must be made as to the most fitting and fruitful approach, and conclusions about theological education will be affected by the one adopted.

For example, if one approaches the church sociologically, the resulting conclusions will encourage preparing leaders who can do well what most ministers spend most of their time doing or what most lay people expect of them. If the approach is through historical theology, the seminaries will need to inject some diversity into their curricula, because these teachings still vary more than do the sociological roles actually filled. Further, because theological doctrines regarding the ministry have not kept pace with historical change, the churches will have to prepare congregations to accept a quite different leadership from that to which they have grown accustomed.

Among the various possibilities for approaching the understanding of the churches in Christian community, we have chosen to take the *world historical approach*. This means, on the one hand, that the church in any locale, but especially in the United States, needs to be informed by awareness of the current global situation. On the other hand, the church as a whole needs to be understood in a comprehensive historical context. What is the place of the church in the history of life on this planet? We hope that this question can be answered in a way that essentially corresponds to the self-understanding of most Christian communities. We hope also that it can be answered in a way that could be acknowledged as correct by persons who are not themselves Christian. That is, an accurate reading of what the Christian church is as a world-historical movement should not preclude an equally accurate understanding of Judaism and Islam or, for that matter, of the other great religious and nonreligious traditions of the world. Roman Catholics and Protestants alike are moving toward such an interpretation, and we believe that the church's basic understanding of theological education should embrace this.

The danger in proposing a world-historical approach to understanding the church is that world history may be assumed to be secularist. This is false; indeed, the idea of world history is itself a product of biblical belief in God, and it fares poorly when it is separated from that belief. For us, placing the church in a world-historical context is placing it in the context of God's creative and redemptive activity. The question is, in what way does the church express, embody, and witness to that activity? We believe that a theological, world-historical approach to understanding the church is essentially biblical, and that it can include what seems most important to most Christians.

A description of the theological world-historical role of the church clearly has normative implications. The church should do well what it fundamentally exists to do. But if what is offered is indeed a description, it must also acknowledge and even emphasize the innumerable sins of the churches. No account of the church's world-historical role can be truthful that does not deal with its persistent and pervasive vilification and persecution of the Jews and its century-long aggression against the Muslims. Also, no account can be truthful that treats these sins as the church's failures to live up to its ideal self-understanding. For these sins have been consistent with some of the ideal images widely held in the church, and much destructive activity of the church, as well as most of its noblest work, has been faithful to such images.

Accordingly, in addition to characterizing the church with regard to its theological world-historical role in this chapter, we shall propose, in Chapter III, images of the church that are informed by the awareness of past sins, appropriate to its role, and rightly directive of its energies today. It is *we* who propose these images as expressive of *our* ideals for the church. We do so, not idiosyncratically, but out of our lifelong participation in the life of the church and our effort to be sensitive to what the church globally is coming to believe about itself. There is nothing sacrosanct about our list, but we hope that it formulates, and can encourage, an emerging worldwide consensus as expressed, for example, in the World Council of Churches.

2. The Church in World History

God has always and everywhere been creatively and redemptively present and working; and she is now and always will be creatively and redemptively active. Her work takes diverse forms according to time, place, and circumstance. It was not the same when cellular life first appeared in the shallow seas as when human beings gradually became distinguished from the other animals. God's work in the prophecies of Amos differed from her work in the teaching of Socrates. And it differs today in a newborn infant and in a mature woman. Thus what God is doing can be understood only in the context of concrete places and times.

For the most part, the work of God is not recognized as such. Recognition was not possible during all the aeons before the appearance of human beings capable of speculative thought and the formation of institutions. Among the early human beings, God's work was seldom acknowledged and often misinterpreted; and even some of the world's great religious traditions do not highlight it or treat it thematically. Furthermore, today in the West, most scholars and intellectuals deny or ignore it.

The appearance of Israel as a community of people who concentrated on God's activity was an event of world-historical significance. Though God works whether or not her activity is recognized, that work takes on new dimensions when human beings acknowledge it and orient their thought and lives to it. Indeed, that acknowledgment and orientation are among God's most important acts! New institutions emerge, and the acknowledgment of God's work takes concrete form in the recollection of the past and the hope for the future. Sacred writings describe her acts, and corporate worship directs the community's attention to them.

The impact of Israel's testimony to God's creative and redemptive activity has now penetrated into almost every corner of the world. What is meant by "God," for good or ill and whether in prayer or derision, has been affected by Israel's recollection and hope. Israel's understanding of history, molded by its particular historical experience and interpretation of God's action, has affected the self-understanding of virtually all educated people. Moreover, the growing concern for human dignity and rights, to which all governments today pay lip service at times, originated mainly in Israel's apprehension of God's work with individual persons. Indeed, the impact of Israel's understanding is evident in the philosophical, political, economic, and ethical thinking of the contemporary world, even where the connection of current ideals to their Jewish origin has been forgotten.

Some of the effect of Israel's history with God has been direct, but it has been widened as a result of two traditions that arose within Israel but then separated themselves: Christianity and Islam. These two religious traditions carried the message of the God known by Israel throughout the world with evangelistic zeal. Even though neither Christianity nor Islam is claimed by the Jewish people as part of their own history, they are still to be seen as part of the impact of Israel on world history.

But our interest here is in Christianity. The crucial figures in its emergence all were Jews who considered themselves as such. Nevertheless, the ministry of the Jewish Jesus, his crucifixion, and the witness to his resurrection by his Jewish disciples introduced controversy into Judaism that led to the separation of those Jews who declared Jesus to be the expected messiah from other Jews. After the second Jerusalem conference, reported in the Book of the Acts of the Apostles, Gentiles were fully received in Christian communities, and this led to further separation. The church became a new institution quite distinct from the synagogue. In fact, the new movement was so successful in the conversion of the Gentiles that by the end of the first century of the Common Era there were Christians who saw themselves as representing the anti-type of Judaism. This separation increasingly has also made the existence of each a theological problem for the other.

As the Christians identified themselves more and more by separation from the Jews, they also drew together into small, tightly knit groups. Those who called themselves Christians were also the people of the churches. At that time almost all persons who were deeply influenced by Jesus were members of the churches, and few were in the churches for any reason other than deeply personal experience of the lordship of Jesus Christ.[1] Indeed, in the early years the church could rightly be thought of as "the body of Christ." Christianity and the church were largely conterminous.

But with the establishment of Christianity in the fourth century, this situation began to change. People little affected by Jesus Christ perceived that being in the church offered them political and social advantages, and so, many became members and identified with Christianity without having entered into a genuine Christian identity themselves. In some cases the church became co-extensive with society, so that those who were born in a given region were assumed to be Christians unless they actively resisted such identification. And as the church added whole peoples to its membership by the edict of their political leaders, discrepancies between church membership and the effective influence of Jesus Christ became quite extreme. There were many thousands of persons baptized by the church who were little affected in their own self-understanding by the teaching of Jesus and the apostolic witness to him.

With the fragmentation of the church, beginning with the Reformation, an opposite distinction between Christianity and the church has arisen. There are now many persons who have deeply assimilated Christian norms and ideals who see no reason to identify with any church. Some even reject the church in the name of Christian principles. Others are indifferent to the church and to the Christian sources of their convictions. As a result, there are millions of persons who are deeply affected by Jesus Christ who do not acknowledge that fact or who acknowledge it and yet choose to remain separate from the church.

For these reasons there are now many inside the churches who manifest little influence of Jesus Christ on their lives and many outside the churches who show marks of being deeply influenced by him. If the church is still the Christian community, therefore, this cannot mean that the church today is the body of Christ in the same sense as it was in the early times. The institutions called churches are certainly not the sole manifestations, or even necessarily the best manifestations, of the presence and effectiveness of Jesus Christ in the world. Also members have no basis for claiming moral superiority.

Likewise, if the church designates itself as "the people of God," that cannot imply that God has worked or is working only in the church. The uniqueness of the church is not that it is exclusively the area of God's activity. Her activity can be perceived in the other biblical traditions as well as among those from Christian cultures who reject the church

---

[1] The fact that conversions were sometimes of whole households could qualify this generalization but not, we think, affect the basic point. See Wayne A. Meeks, *The First Urban Christians* (New Haven, CT: Yale University Press, 1983).

because of its sins. Beyond that, God was working in the world before human life appeared on it, and she has certainly continued to work in all human communities.

Nevertheless, there remains a role for Christianity to play alongside Judaism and Islam. All three witness to Israel's history with God and all discern the meaning and relevance of that history in our time. All acknowledge that God's work with Israel was her work with her people for the sake of the whole world.[2] It is this recollection of the history of Israel as the people of God that enables the continuing affirmation that God has worked creatively and redemptively in the world. This heightens the hope and expectation that God is now working and will continue to work within the world and for the world.

Although Judaism, Christianity, and Islam thus have much in common, they are far from identical. Each witnesses to Israel's life with God in its own way. Christianity is that movement within human history in which the efficacy of Israel's witness to God's creative and redemptive work has been mediated through Jesus and the apostolic witness to God's activity in him. This witness affirms not only the activity of God in the world but also her loving forgiveness and acceptance of all those sinners for whom Jesus died, that is, all human beings. Just as God's creative and redemptive work goes on whether acknowledged or not, so also the efficacy of Jesus and the forgiving love of God do not depend on being recognized. But just as the recognition of God's work is a gift of God that has enhanced the effectiveness of her work, so also grateful acceptance of God's forgiveness is essential for its full effectiveness. Likewise, without the acknowledgment and celebration of Jesus, the influence of Jesus in the world would have been trivial. Therefore the means whereby the memory of Jesus is kept alive is of great importance.

By far the most effective means of keeping this memory alive has been the telling of the story and its enactment in the Eucharist. Scripture, sermon, and sacrament are central. Where communities gather for word and sacrament, there is the church. The church is the community which in these ways keeps alive the memory of Israel's life with God as perceived in and through Jesus and the apostolic witness to him. In its witness, and especially in the sacramental representation of Jesus' death and resurrection, the church discerns the creative and redemptive activity of God.

This understanding of the church entails no claim for its moral and spiritual virtue. The community that keeps alive the memory of Jesus may at some times and places be more interested in self-aggrandizement than in living as that memory directs. But this understanding of the

[2] Rolf Knierim, "The Task of Old Testament Theology," *Horizons in Biblical Theology*, Vol. 6, No. 1, June 1984, pp. 25–27.

church does indicate its importance. Apart from the church, the other manifestations of Christianity in our world would fade rapidly, and apart from Christianity, a large part of the world would not participate in the hope grounded in the memory and discernment of God's creative and redemptive activity.

3. *The Internal History of the Church*

Thus far we have spoken of Jesus as mediator to Gentiles of Israel's knowledge of God. After millenia of claiming that Christian knowledge superseded that of the Jews, rendering it truncated or false, it would be wise for Christians to place the emphasis here. But there are also distinctive emphases in the Christian understanding of Israel's God based on the conviction that God was creatively and redemptively present and active in the life, death, and resurrection of Jesus. The Christian memory of God's activity and of Israel's witness to that activity is stamped by the figure of the crucified and risen one through whom Christians came to this knowledge. Christian discernment of God's present activity and forgiving love, and Christian hope for the future, are also informed by this distinctive perspective. This fact has often led to claims for Christian superiority or even absoluteness, but it need not do so. H. Richard Niebuhr in *The Meaning of Revelation* showed us how Christians can testify with conviction and power to their experience of God through Jesus without passing pejorative judgments on the experience of other communities.[3]

In this chapter we shall not summarize how the figure of Jesus shapes the knowledge of God of those who have come to know God through him; the images of the church in Chapter III will indicate what is entailed. But in order to underscore the understanding of the church as the community that keeps alive the memory of Jesus and, through him, of Israel, we shall say something more about how the church is constituted in relation to this memory. And what we say will be heavily influenced by Niebuhr's book.

The church is distinguished from all other institutions by its central act of celebrating and renewing the memory of Jesus. This kind of memory is what Niebuhr calls *internal history*. All communities find their identity in a shared internal history. Americans share the stories of Jamestown, the Pilgrim Fathers, and the Revolutionary War. These are told as *our* stories; and to be an American is to accept them as our stories. This is quite independent of whether one's biological ancestors were actually present at Jamestown or Plymouth or were supporters of the American Revolution. In contrast, an external history might correctly trace the ancestry of most contemporary citizens of the United States to

---

[3] H. Richard Niebuhr, *The Meaning of Revelation* (New York: Macmillan, 1941).

persons who were in Europe, Africa, Latin America, or Asia at the time of these events. But to whatever extent United States citizenship gives people their identity, these ancient events become part of their internal history. The public schools, public holidays, and political speeches do much to inculcate this identity through these stories.

Likewise, to whatever extent people's individual or corporate identity is Christian, it is because of their incorporation into the internal history told and celebrated in the Christian church. Christians are among those who know that wherever their biological ancestors may have been, their true ancestors were wandering Arameans, slaves in Egypt, freed and given the land of Canaan. They read the stories of Abraham and Sarah, of Jacob and Rachel, of Mary and Joseph, of St. John of the Cross and St. Teresa of Avila as those of their forefathers and foremothers in the faith. Christians read the stories of Christian saints, martyrs, and missionaries as their history. One is objectively a part of the Christian movement today to the extent that one is subjectively influenced by this history. Thus one has Christian identity to the extent that one claims this history as one's own.

There is always the danger that internal history will be idealized and falsified and that external threats to the community identified by this history will be villified and demonized. Indeed, there are few who have not succumbed to this temptation. Yet, what is remarkable about Israel is not that occasionally this tendency is apparent there, too, but that the sins of its heroes and the virtues of its enemies are not concealed. Because Israel acknowledged the activity of God as primary, it could remember the rebelliousness of its own response without destroying its identity. That possibility was bequeathed to Christianity and remains normative for it, although Christians have historically been more guilty than Jews have of falsely idealizing their heroes and demonizing their enemies. Nevertheless, the memory of Jesus, as well as the Jewish scriptures mediated to the church through him, condemn this aberration.

When Christian identity is established so that its internal history can be acknowledged for what it is, Christians have nothing to fear from external history. On the contrary, they want to learn whatever they can about themselves and those whom they accept as their mothers and fathers in the faith. It is painful to realize that those who have been most admired have often been vicious in their anti-Judaism, but Christian identity cannot be shaken by this. That identity is based on seeing what God can do and has done through sinful human beings, now upon a line of heroes who are free of vice. The grace of God, and not the works of human beings, is the theme of the Christian story.

Christian identity exists outside the fellowship of the church. Especially among individuals who find the church boring or fixed on irrelevant or damaging ideas and practices, Christian identity is often strong.

But cut off from the fellowship of the community that nurtures and celebrates that identity, it withers and is rarely passed from generation to generation. Christian identity depends upon the church. The Church is constituted by its responsibility for making effective the memory and the resulting anticipation of God's creative and redemptive activity.

4. *Distortions of Christian Identity*

In describing the role of the church in a theological world-historical context, it has been necessary to acknowledge the depth and scope of its anti-Jewish teaching and practice. Christians can thank God for their liberation to self-knowledge about this sin without in any way excusing or justifying it. They also seek the truth about themselves in other areas as well, however painful it may be.

The most important of these other sins is misogyny. There may have been positive reasons in the dialectics of history for imaging God as male and even for a period of male dominance in the shaping of religious institutions. But whether or not such a historical defense is possible, the exploitation of women by men allowed and even affirmed by Judaism and Christianity is inexcusable. Furthermore, the failure of official teaching to take women's experience into account and the exclusion of women from an equal role in leadership have been massive sins against women, against the whole church, and against God.

If a Christian identity can be reaffirmed in the context of the honest recognition of Christian misogyny, it must be by a fresh reading of Christian history through the centrality of Jesus.[4] Such a reading demands that its internal history be radically reconstituted. Much that has been proudly told must be confessed as sin; and much that has been obscured and silenced must be given voice. In particular the immense contribution of women, despite their second-class status in the church, can be told with joy.

The language we use in our worship must also change. The time when male imagery for God appropriately dominated, if it ever existed, is now past. In this book we speak of God as "she" because we believe it important to break damaging habits of mind. Of course, God is no more female than male, but the destructive power of predominantly male images will not disappear until such habits are broken.

Even when Christian identity is not formed in opposition to another community, it shares with all group identity certain dangers. The determination of who "we" are separates "us" from those "others" who are not part of this determination. Because this is inevitable, it must be regarded

---

[4] Elizabeth Schüssler Fiorenza has shown that the impact of Jesus disrupted patriarchal patterns in some of the earliest Christian communities. Cf. *In Memory of Her* (New York: Crossroad, 1983).

in some sense as morally neutral. In the Christian case there is a tendency to acknowledge "them" as also being the children of God and those for whom Jesus died. There is, therefore, an inherent check against a competitive spirit that rejoices in "our" victories over "them" and against the supposition that "we" are by nature superior to "them."

This check has been important in Christian history, but it has not been completely successful. Instead, there has been a strong tendency toward a "we-they" thinking in which the "they" are demonized or viewed as fundamentally inferior. Furthermore, this general human tendency toward tribalism has been closely associated with a racism that has *no* basis in the New Testament. As Christianity lost out to Islam in most of Asia and Africa, European Christians increasingly associated Christianity with their European culture and race. Although few altogether rejected the universalizing tendency of Christianity, many have thought of that as universalizing white Western Christianity without questioning the close connection of Christianity with whiteness and Western culture. Africans and Asians who became Christian were expected to adopt white, Western ways and even white, Western images of Jesus and of God. It is only as the victims of these partly unconscious habits of mind have forced attention to these distortions that white, Western Christians are beginning to rid themselves of this tribalization of their faith.

5. *The Expansion of Christian Identity—Internalizing Eternal History*

Although Christian identity is always determined by an internal history centering on Jesus and the apostolic witness to him, its content and valuation are continually changing. Sometimes this change takes a different form from any expressed above. An example is found in the relations of Protestants and Catholics. Niebuhr wrote in 1941:

> There will be no union of Catholics and Protestants until through the common memory of Jesus Christ the former repent of the sin of Peter and the latter of the sin of Luther, until Protestants acknowledge Thomas Aquinas as one of their fathers, the Inquisition as their own sin and Ignatius Loyola as one of their own Reformers, until Catholics have canonized Luther and Calvin, done repentance for Protestant nationalism, and appropriated Schleiermacher and Barth as their theologians.[5]

To the astonishment of the world, by 1965 this change in the Roman Catholics' internal history had begun. In the past two decades, though they have not literally canonized Luther and Calvin (God forbid!), they have come to treat them with great respect and have joined with Protestants in celebrating the five-hundredth anniversary of Luther's birth. And they

[5] Niebuhr, op. cit., p. 119.

have appropriated Schleiermacher and Barth as their theologians.

Protestants have moved more slowly and erratically. Few have internalized the Council of Trent, but Thomas and Ignatius are widely appreciated as a part of the shared Christian heritage, and there are signs elsewhere of a slow merging of memories. In many contexts the alienation that characterized Protestants and Catholics twenty years ago has given way to a unity as strong as that joining Protestants across denominational boundaries.

The broadening of internal history can also be achieved by overcoming a strictly linear view of history. Historians have long pointed out the many streams that flowed together to make up Jewish life and faith: Persian, Mesopotamian, Canaanite, and Egyptian ideas and practices all contributed, as well as, in later times, Hellenistic ones. But Christians tend to trace their internal history through a single line and to view other influences as external. Yet they need not do so. Christians, too, can learn to appreciate Persians, Mesopotamians, Canaanites, Egyptians, and Hellenists, as well as Jews, as forefathers and foremothers in their faith.

This pattern of multiple influence does not end with Jesus. On the contrary, the apostolic witness and the Christian community continued to draw on many traditions. The Greek philosophers made their contribution to the emergent church alongside the Jewish scriptures and new Christian writings. Despite much conflict, the catholic spirit affirmed the classical sources of wisdom, and Plato and Cicero became part of the internal history of Christendom.

The point to be made and underscored is that Christian identity does not require that all events lying outside the line of Yahwistic Judaism and Jesus-centered Christianity be viewed externally. In these events, too, can be discerned the creative and redemptive work of God. On the other hand, this does not mean that all events in the past can play an equal role in determining Christian identity. For internal history to have coherence it must be ordered around one center—an idea, a principle, an angle of vision, or an event. For the Christian it will always be finally an event—the event of Jesus' life, death, and resurrection. This event will always have its meaning in large part as mediating the story of Jesus' people, the Jews. It is only in and through the particularity of this event and that history that the multiple sources of those events and the wider course of history can also be appropriated as internal history.

However, this is not a restriction. On the contrary, Israel's history with God, viewed through Jesus Christ, has its setting in universal history and opens us to discern the creative and redemptive work of God everywhere. When the center is Jesus Christ, in principle every circumference we draw that leaves out part of God's world is artificial and false. Individuals can achieve wholeness only as these barriers crumble. As Niebuhr wrote:

> To remember all that is in our past and so in our present is to achieve unity of self. To remember the human past as our own past is to achieve community with mankind. Such conversion of the memory is an important, indispensable part of the soul's conversion. Without the integration of the personal and social past there can be no present integrity of the self nor anything like human brotherhood. Through Jesus Christ, Christians can and must turn again and again to history, making the sins and the faiths of their fathers and brothers their own faiths and sins.[6]

But if this talk of expanding our internal history is not to be a platitude or a dream, its implications for today must be examined. One of these pertains to the relation of Christians to the religious heritage of India and East Asia. Does a Christian identity lead to viewing Hinduism, Buddhism, Jainism, Taoism, and Confucianism as external—as rivals to Christianity? Or, for example, can an internal history centering in Jesus Christ include also Gautama Buddha? If this inclusiveness is not possible, Christian claims to the universal relevance and meaning of the salvific and revelatory act of God in Jesus require revision. The voices of those who call on Christians to give up Christocentrism will have to be heeded.[7] But we are not prepared to make this move. We believe that the great sages and spiritual giants of China and India can become part of the internal history centered in Jesus Christ just as Plato and Seneca did. Indeed, we believe that this is already happening.

Yet this cannot be a matter of mere expansion. Gautama, like Jesus, has universal meaning for a theological history of the world, and an internal history that includes him will be transformed throughout. The identity created by this Buddha-influenced internal history will be new, but because it will center in Jesus Christ and because it is through this centrality that this expansion and transformation have been made possible and necessary, it will be a new Christian identity. Indeed, it will be a more fully Christian identity, because it will have realized more of the universality and inclusiveness always grasped by believers in principle in the Christ event but so often turned into false claims to universality on the part of very parochial forms of Christianity.

Needless to say, the expansion and transformation of Christian identity by the expansion and transformation of internal history to include Buddhist history does not entail the expansion of the church to include all Buddhists as members. The effect on Buddhists of such an expansion and transformation of the self-understanding of the church remains to be seen. It would mean, however, that for Buddhists as individuals or as communities to enter the church would not entail uprooting from the internal history by which they have lived or the rejection of their previous identity. It

---

[6] Ibid., pp. 117–18.
[7] Tom F. Driver, *Christ in a Changing World* (New York: Crossroad, 1981).

would mean instead that they had found in Jesus Christ a center within which that history and identity could be included in a larger whole. On the other hand, instead of finding a new center in Jesus, Buddhists may seek to make more concrete their own universal claims for Buddha by showing how from that center the real historical meaning of Israel's life with God can be included. The result would be a profound transformation of Buddhism. In either case, the Christian witness to the universal and saving truth in Jesus Christ will have been an important gift to the Buddhist community.

6. *Christian Identity and the Enlightenment*

The most important recent developments in the identity of North American Anglo-Saxon Protestants have been those associated with modernity. Even the Reformation is less important for the self-understanding of most Protestants. The great missionary movement arising in the nineteenth century associated the gospel with the fruits of modernity: democracy, human rights, education for all, scientific medicine, and, in general, the application of modern technology to meeting human needs. Although we realize that there are other currents in North American Protestantism to which much of what we will say in this section is less directly relevant, notably the Black church, all theological education must reexamine itself in relation to this history.

Of course, not all Protestants have accepted all aspects of modernity as normative. Some conservatives have clung to features of the pre-modern world view, such as the separate creation of the human race. But even for these conservatives the terms of the debate are set by shared elements in the modern mind. The debate about the supernatural, for example, largely assumed modern notions of the natural. The question was whether, given a fully natural universe from which God is absent, some events are caused by divine intervention. The conservative view that there are such events is as far removed from biblical understanding as is the modernist, since it is based on a modern understanding of nature rather than on the biblical vision of God's creative and redemptive activity in all the world.

The rise of modernity in the Renaissance and its victory in the Enlightenment were often tied to the struggle against clericalism, the church as a whole, and even Christianity. Nevertheless, in broad perspective, it was a development within the stream of Western Christian history, and it has been largely assimilated into the inner history of Protestants in the United States. Even conservatives often see such proponents of the Enlightenment vision as George Washington, Benjamin Franklin, and Thomas Jefferson as respected forefathers. Since most of the ideas of the Enlightenment are rooted in the biblical tradition and in its subsequent development by Christian theologians, including the Protestant Reformers, even the assimilation of the criticisms of Christian institutions, practices, and ideas has not been difficult.

In the past, most of the Christian resistance to the Enlightenment has been to its threat to scriptural and ecclesiastical authority and to particular traditional doctrines. That situation is now changing as modernity itself is losing its confidence.[8]

The modern dualism of human beings or minds on the one side and nature on the other no longer seems conceptually adequate, and its damaging consequences in practice are widely recognized. The further fragmentation of the sciences is linked to a general loss of the Enlightenment belief in the capacity of the human mind to apprehend reality. The strong individualism of the Enlightenment in which Protestants have taken so much pride now appears to be a major cause of our social problems. Whereas the loss of confidence in Christian identity had long been associated with the criticism of the church for its resistance to the Enlightenment, it now is equally connected with the criticism of the church for its sacralization of Enlightenment emphases. The contemporary North American church therefore must reconsider this part of its internal history.

Perhaps the main element that separates the Enlightenment from premodern expressions of otherwise similar ideas is the prestige of natural science and the distinctive world view that has accompanied it. This science, like the Enlightenment in general, is both a product and an opponent of Western Christianity. Only recently has it become clear how tightly theological ideas were woven into this modern science. David Griffin has gathered the results of this historical research, and the following summary is based on his work.[9]

Three movements struggled for supremacy during the seventeenth century: the fading power of Aristotelian philosophy, the rising power of the "magical" vision, and the emerging power of mechanist thinking. The last eventually won out, and, accordingly, history has been written as if it were *the* scientific world view responsible for all the great achievements of science. The actual evidence, long resisted and even concealed by the advocates of the mechanist world view, is that the magical movement provided the impetus for the rise of modern science.

This movement drew on the traditions of Pythagoras, Plato, Neoplatonism, Hermetic mysticism, and the Kabala. It was fascinated by number, and it turned to mathematics and science as the earlier Latin

---

[8] Cf. Leslie Newbigen, *The Other Side of 1984* (Geneva: World Council of Churches, 1983).

[9] David Griffin, "Theological Education and the Rise of Modern Science" (unpublished manuscript, 1983).

Renaissance had not. Ficino, Paracelsus, and Bruno were among its early leaders. It inspired Kepler and Francis Bacon as well.

The Aristotelian tradition had emphasized the teleological element in all things. The magical tradition went far beyond this. It sought to ally itself with spiritual forces immanent in all things so as to bend them to human use and control. For it, nature was alive with spirit, and the explanations of natural events were to be found in these immanent spiritual forces, which could act at a distance as well as in proximity.

The primary objection to this tradition was not that it inhibited scientific investigation or blinded its adherents to empirical data. It did not. The primary objection was that it threatened belief in a God who transcended nature as its omnipotent creator. This was also associated with undermining the acceptance of hierarchical authority in human affairs. By seeing a miraculous aspect in all natural events, it weakened the appeal to miracles by which the Catholic church argued for its authority. It was for this reason that Mersenne, the senior correspondent of Descartes, favored Aristotelianism over the magical tradition, but saw even more promise in mechanism. Robert Boyle opposed the magical tradition because it united God with matter in a theologically unacceptable way. Accordingly, he denied to creatures any power to move themselves, attributing all power of motion to the external, omnipotent God. To him, the created world was purely objective matter, completely passive in relation to God.

Newton was influenced by both the magical and the materialist traditions, but for theological reasons he moved to the materialist camp. By denuding nature of all power of self-motion, he magnified the power of God. In gravity Newton found action at a distance that was rejected by the strict mechanists and seemed to support the proponents of magic. In explaining gravity, he refused to allow any mechanist account such as that of Descartes. There was no physical connection, he argued, between distant bodies. But Newton ridiculed the idea that material bodies at a distance could exercise any influence on each other. The explanation had to be based on spiritual forces external to the material objects, ultimately, God. Thus, again, Newton glorified divine power by denying power to the creatures.

The emergence of materialism, which denied to nature any purpose, capacity for self-movement, or interiority, was not essential to science. It succeeded because it gave support to theological voluntarism, the idea that the transcendent God imposes by fiat "His" will upon the world. In time the mechanist account of how matter operated became so satisfactory to many people that they freed mechanist materialism from its original association with the imposed will of God. A world composed of purely material, and therefore purely passive, entities became completely self-sufficient. Ironically, this mechanistic materialism came to be known as the Newtonian world view.

This mechanistic-materialist world view was never adequate to the evidence, but its success in guiding theory formation and experimentation was so great that it became entrenched as common sense. When Hume undercut it empirically, Kant reestablished it as grounded in the universal structure of mind. When it became impossible any longer to apply this world view to subatomic physics, much of the scientific and philosophical community concluded that thinkers were condemned to paradox and unintelligibility, and for that reason remained firmly identified with mechanistic materialism. Even those who, after generations of erosion of its scientific viability, acknowledge that it may not be objectively true as a world view still usually insist that there is no other methodological alternative than to assume it.

The rejection of the magical view of nature in favor of the materialist one, so fateful for the shaping of modernity, was, to put it more technically, a rejection of internal relations. The units of matter were to be viewed as entities that relate to one another only externally in terms of pushes and pulls. In their own individual being they remain unaffected by these relations. More generally, these units, in contrast with those of the magical vision, have no inner reality at all. They exist only for observers or as they exercise force on others. Nature is purely objective. A tree or a dog is a complex machine—nothing more.

Although some people have extended this mechanical nature to include human beings as well, and this has greatly affected scientific research on human beings, the general Enlightenment teaching has been dualistic. Descartes established a dualism of mind and matter at the base of modern philosophy, and although the history of modern philosophy may be read as a struggle with and against the conceptual problems that it entailed, dualist modes of thought have widely prevailed. The human mind is contrasted with the pure objectivity and pure passivity of the natural world. Nevertheless, in one important respect the human mind was seen as analogous to the units of nature. Each mind is a self-contained individual. In Descartes' terms, like the units of nature, it is a substance, which means that it requires nothing but itself for its existence. The world view associated with the victorious science supported individualism, and the political, social, and economic theories (and practices) that arose during the Enlightenment reflect that individualism. And at least in the English-speaking world and its churches, these theories are still prevalent.

German idealism belongs to the Enlightenment in its acceptance of its view of nature and the dualism of nature and mind. Its reflection on human mind, however, led away from individualism. Human mind, or *Geist*, can be conceived as a unitary reality in which individual human minds participate. It has its own structure, and its history is not simply the result of what myriad individual human beings do. On the contrary, individuals have their existence and meaning in their relation to the history of *Geist*. Marx shifted attention from the history of culture and thought to the history of economic life, but he retained this general sense that individual life has its being and meaning in a history that is governed by its own laws.

German idealism and its Marxist offspring are of obvious importance to today's world, but they are not a significant part of the internal history and identity of North American Protestant churches. For this reason we shall only mention this antithetical tradition and set it aside. We shall refer to the Enlightenment as it originated in the seventeenth and eighteenth centuries and has continued to inform the English-speaking world.

7. Enlightenment Individualism and Its Consequences

Alisdair McIntyre has spoken of the "invention" of the Enlightenment as the individual who is wholly subject and sovereign in matters of truth.[10] His primary concern is with the problem that individualism created for ethics. When the individual is the sole arbiter of truth, to what standard does one appeal in order to justify moral decisions? Indeed, it becomes difficult to discern any concrete way in which one can arbitrate conflicting truth claims of any sort.

Given this individualism, it is hardly surprising that the dominant strain of democratic political theory is contractualism. If individuals decide for themselves what is true and good, then they alone will also decide on matters of political consent that are the bases for democratic associations. Having given some sort of implied or expressed consent, the individual, to be sure, agrees in principle to obey the rules of order established by the majority of the consenting individuals within the association. Yet there are certain individual rights that are protected, and if they are seriously violated, the contract can be invalidated again by individual choice.

Economic theory, also, held the desires and decisions of the individual as primary. In general it was argued that individuals seek their own interest and maximize their own profits. Instead of deploring this selfishness, economists showed how it led to efficiency and growth in the economy as a whole. Efforts by the state to intervene by restricting individual initiative and freedom interfere with the rational production and distribution of goods and slow down the development of business and industry. Hence the wisest policy of governments is laissez-faire. And those individuals who work most diligently for their personal interests are at the same time those who make the greatest contribution to the good of

10 McIntyre, op. cit., p. 59.

the whole. Although economists have recognized the need of some government control to prevent monopoly, for example, or to sustain those who fail in the competition, the individualism manifest in the foundation of modern economic theory still prevails.

The internalization of Enlightenment individualism by Christians has deeply affected the understanding of the church as well. It has also caused some serious problems for the concept of the people of God in mission. Individuals do "join" the church, but because American churches, regardless of their official polity, function as voluntary associations, they are mostly congeries of consenting individuals whose commitment to the church is very conditional.

Furthermore, the understanding of salvation is thoroughly individual. It is, in traditional language, the individual soul that is to be saved. Where this language has declined, what has replaced it is an essentially individualistic psychology. People now attend church to have their personal needs met, and psychology governs the programs in education and in counseling. Even the principal content of preaching is now psychological.

The contemporary interest in spirituality only further expresses and reinforces this pervasive individualism. Recognizing the limits of secular psychology, sensitive Christians are searching deeper. But the depths they are exploring are individual depths.

Individualism has been the ideology of the bourgeoisie. It has strengthened their hand against established authorities. It has justified their claim for political rights. And it has freed them from moral restraint in their pursuit of economic goals. Those who lack the economic basis for exercising their political rights are also denied the economic security of traditional society and become fair game for exploitation by the bourgeoisie.

The bourgeoisie have dominated the church as well as society since the Enlightenment. Thus the Christian tradition has been controlled by the interests of those who live well, or at least relatively well. The interests of persons like these are, of course, not to be ignored. However, the middle and upper classes have so dominated Christianity that its institutional forms and even its theology reflect those interests almost to the exclusion of the large masses of the poor and dispossessed.[11] Even the powerful theological virtue of charity did not survive the dominance of bourgeois mentality. It was domesticated and in practice reduced to the giving of alms. Thus nothing changed except that the givers felt righteous. The poor remained poor, the rich remained rich, and all remained in their stations and performed their duties.

Perhaps the finest statement of an alternative to both individualism and collectivism is that by Dietrich Bonhoeffer. In his book *Sanctorum Communio*, Bonhoeffer argues that at its base, human reality is social.

[11] Johann Metz, *The Emergent Church*, trans. Peter Mann (New York: Crossroad, 1981).

Relying heavily on contemporary sociological thought, Bonhoeffer contends that the self is constituted by its relation to others in the community. The individual, furthermore, is always a self in a community that unites all human communities into one universal community with God.[12]

Political theologians in Germany and liberation theologians in Latin America have led the way to implement this alternative vision of human reality as profoundly social. They have done so with more attention to the actual class structure and system of oppression than Bonhoeffer offered. Much of what they say echoes themes familiar in North America from the days of the social gospel. Their call, like that of the social gospel, for corporate salvation is obviously rooted in the Bible and in church history. It overcomes individualism without oppressing individuals. We have thus only to return to major, if not dominant, currents in our internal history in order to assimilate the insights we are now receiving.

But even if the theological task is well advanced, much other theoretical work remains to be done. We must clarify the nature of ethics, political theory, or economics based on a genuinely social understanding of human beings. Otherwise we shall continue to be forced largely to choose between capitalist individualism and Marxist collectivism or some compromise between them. If the church has an alternative vision for its own life, it needs to share this with the larger society.

In any case it is a long way from the availability of suitable ideas to their internalization in the lives of the North American churches, which are organized around a concern for personal salvation. They emphasize that saved individuals will be concerned about the wider world and will act for its sake. They recognize the importance of structural change to realize the justice that is required. But the salvation that expresses itself secondarily in the concern for social issues is first and foremost personal. In the dominant view the church's life is primarily for the sake of persons, and only secondarily to enable persons to act for the sake of society. Indeed "secondary" becomes very secondary when the controversial character of social action appears.

In Latin America the response to the church's control by the individualistic understanding of salvation has been the creation of thousands of base communities dedicated to salvation as corporate liberation. Nothing like that seems possible in the United States and Canada. The pendulum is swinging away from such limited activity as the church has had in the past for the sake of what Dorothee Soelle calls "the indivisible salvation of the whole world."[13] An alternative structuring of the church for the sake of such salvation, with the partial exception of the Black church, has hardly yet been envisaged.

[12] Dietrich Bonhoeffer, *Sanctorum Communio* (New York: Harper & Row, 1963).
[13] Dorothee Soelle, *Political Theology* (Philadelphia: Fortress Press, 1974).

Perhaps North American society cannot now sustain any church other than an individually oriented one. Perhaps any Christian communities in the United States and Canada that do structure themselves for the sake of the indivisible salvation of the whole world must remain peripheral to the Christian movement. Nevertheless, their existence can offer Christianity a reminder of the fragmentary character of its present life. It can help keep alive those aspects of Christianity's inner history that the dominant church neglects and conceals. It can thereby sustain and increase the appreciation of the creative and redemptive activity of God through other segments of Christianity even when this activity takes the form of judgment upon the church.

Contemporary North American Protestantism is fundamentally conservative. It seeks in Christianity the sanction for and the sanctification of received cultural values and structures. In this respect it is not different from most of the forms of Christianity that preceded it, at least since the time of Constantine. The difference is that today what is sanctioned and sanctified is largely the individualistic heritage of the Enlightenment.

Sociologically this is easy to understand. Established institutions support the basic structures of the society in which they are established. In remembering our inner history, we can distinguish between the behavior of the established church and the implications of its teaching. We can discuss whether the advantage of being established, legally or socially, outweighs the disadvantage of allying with other established structures. We can take pride in the rare case of Medellin in which an established church, at least in part, allied itself with the oppressed against the political and economic structures of oppression.[14]

Yet the problem is as much theological as it is sociological. Even if the church proclaims its solidarity with the oppressed, difficulties will remain because of conflict at the farthest level between Christian belief and certain revolutionary necessities. For example, the love of enemies is problematical because revolutionary energies are often better mobilized by hate. Reconciliation, a notion at the heart of Christian faith, seems premature to those who are swamped by injustice. Opposition to violence seems hypocritical when it does not oppose the systemic violence of oppressive structures.

Perhaps even more fundamentally, the Christian teaching regarding human sinfulness as rooted more deeply than what revolution can affect makes some Christians pessimistic about the possibility of realizing justice in society. Thus those utopian hopes that are so important to the

---

[14] In a 1968 meeting at Medellin, the Conference of Latin American Bishops clearly affirmed that the church is for the poor. Most of them then, no doubt, did not realize the full implications of what they did. It has led to important changes in the role and image of the Roman Catholic Church in Latin America.

generation of revolutionary fervor are discouraged by traditional Christian theology. Even when it is critical of the status quo and supportive of those who would change it, the church's teaching sometimes weakens the will of those who alone would be able to overthrow it. If violent revolution is the only path to liberation, then Christian teaching itself appears as an obstacle to liberation. The Marxists insist that they must take the lead in seeking the indivisible salvation of the whole world.

This dilemma is a real one for Christians. They cannot give up their emphasis on love and reconciliation. Their skepticism of human virtue and the purity of justice achieved by violent revolutions is too well founded to be set aside. But of the alternative evils among which they must choose, the violent overthrow of a social system may be the least evil. Christian thinkers have already attempted to extend just-war theory to popular revolutions.[15] In practice, revolutions are being more and more often approved by Christians in the name of love and justice.

What is becoming clear is that intolerable structures of injustice can no longer be rationalized by sentimental appeals to individualistic love that imply passivity in the face of that oppression. In a conflict, there is little middle ground. One is either for or against those who are protesting injustice. The church is confronted with the unsavory record of its past and must begin to think in new ways about its current practices in the face of the worldwide protests against exploitation and repression.

8. Enlightenment Dualism and Its Consequences

Next to individualism, dualism may be to North American Christians the most pervasive and pernicious legacy of the Enlightenment. It was readily assimilated, as dualistic tendencies were already present in the tradition. Indeed, Descartes derived his vision of a dichotomy between mind and matter from the Western tradition, with its roots in both the Bible and Greek philosophy. But in those traditions, the tendencies toward dualism were embedded in ideas that eased the dichotomy if it did not eradicate it. For example, there was the vision of the great chain of being, notions of world soul, and a sense of organism as more fundamental than mechanism. Descartes systematized dualistic tendencies in the tradition into absolutes.

Descartes recognized that there were conceptual problems with dualism, and these were extensively considered by the philosophers of the Enlightenment. But our concern here is more with dualism's social and existential consequences. We shall begin with the dualism of mind

---

[15] Cf. Karoly Proehle, "Revolution as a Question for Christian Ethics," *Luther World*, Vol. 16, No. 1, 1969, pp. 29–46. See also Joseph Hough, "The Christian, Violence and Social Change," in Norman Brockman and Nicholas Piediscalzi, eds., *Contemporary Religion and Social Responsibility*, pp. 23ff.

and body and then consider the wider implications of the dualism of history and nature.

Sociologically, the mind-body dualism functioned in the bourgeois imagination to exalt the bourgeois individual as mind and to view those who were unable to realize their individuality as matter. Of course, the official rhetoric attributed mind to all human beings, and this softened the tendency of which we speak. But psychologically and sociologically, it is clear that the individualistic respect for individuals did not extend to the classes and races exploited by capitalism. Instead of effectively realizing the humanistic ideals of the Enlightenment, dualism consciously or unconsciously justified colonialism and even slavery.

Furthermore, in actual operation, the free individuals of Enlightenment rhetoric were the males. Women were effectively excluded from developing their individuality and were treated as belonging to the side of body rather than mind. Because intrinsic value belonged only to mind, the categorization of people as bodies reduced them to the status of mere means to the ends of those who were truly individual minds.

The negative effects of mind-body dualism were not limited to those who were cast in the role of bodies. Those who understood themselves as minds also suffered, for the implication of this sort of dualism is alienation from the body. One's own body is a machine with which one is incidentally linked. It is to be used for one's purposes but is not allowed to lay claims upon one. One's achievement as a person is measured by one's success in subduing and controlling one's body. This may lead either to asceticism or to exploiting the body for the pleasures one thereby attains. But because the body's value lies only in its service to the mind, one is not likely to care for it tenderly or to be sensitive to learning from its wisdom.

Alienation from the body also includes alienation from sexuality. This can lead to the repression of sexuality or to its exploitation for pleasure. In neither case does this encourage a tender human relation with a sexual partner. Instead, it degrades the partner—the woman—to an object. In the context of dualism, sexuality is connected more with pornography and violence than with affection and love.

The antipathy of the mind toward the body has led to repression, hypocrisy, and self-deceit. It has focused the understanding of sin upon actions that are often both natural and healthy and has identified "morality" with the avoidance of these actions. It has often led to projections onto others, especially onto women and people of other classes and races, of "sins" that one dares not acknowledge as one's own. It has produced great personal misery and destructive feelings of guilt, and therefore it has made impossible any full integration of human personality.

This Enlightenment dualism expressed and reinforced the long association of Christianity with asceticism, which has inspired repeated revolts. The insistence on the domination of mind or spirit over the body has led in reaction to the total rejection of the spirit for the sake of the body. The salvation or wholeness that has been sought by Christians through the suppression of normal bodily wants has been sought by others through the glorification of sexuality as the one avenue of human fulfillment. A society obsessed with sex because of its repression has been transformed into a society obsessed with sex as the instrument of its salvation. These reversals express the continued power of dualism.

When the church repents of the dualistic opposition of mind to body or spirit to sexuality, it can find positive resources in the Bible. Israel accepted sexuality as natural and good and was far less preoccupied with it than Christians were. Indeed, Judaism as a whole has never succumbed to the dualism so characteristic of Christian teaching. The New Testament also gives far less support to this dualism than Christians have long supposed. Paul's hostility toward the flesh was not directed especially toward sexuality. His recommendation of celibacy was connected with his apocalyptic expectations rather than with a dualistic opposition to the body.

Nevertheless, these problems cannot easily be resolved. To be led by the sexual revolution to recognize the evil of our sexual asceticism should not mean the uncritical affirmation of all aspects of the revolution. The recognition that sexuality is good and belongs to human wholeness should not mean that it can dominate human wholeness or provide the principle of human integration. Along with all other aspects of life, it must be subordinated to the ends to which God calls us. That means that sexual discipline remains important. All things are permitted, but not all things are profitable or appropriate. Christians do not ask what they are morally allowed to do but rather how they may order all aspects of their lives toward the realization of God's purposes. They have not learned how to affirm together the goodness and cleanness of sexuality and the importance of sexual discipline for the sake of larger purposes. They have, as a church, no convincing word to say on this most intimate and universal of human problems. Until Christians become genuinely free from dualistic ways of thinking, the church will not find its voice.

For Descartes this dualism was only incidentally that of the mind and the human body. Primarily the matter from which the mind was distinguished was the nonhuman world. This Descartes understood geometrically. For him, as for modern science generally, biology would one day be interpreted as a special case of mathematical physics. Plants and animals were as much a part of the world machine as were rocks and planets. Thus, whereas the effects of dualism were ambiguous with respect to women and to subordinated races and classes, they were unequivocally negative with respect to other living things, which are nothing but matter. The appearance that animals suffer pain is only an appearance. There is no difference between a whining dog and a squeaking door, and concern for the happiness of an animal is a false sentiment.

Not all Enlightenment thinkers followed Descartes explicitly on this point. A deeper common sense, that other animals are subjects of experience somewhat as we are, was never eradicated from the modern consciousness. But it was effectively suppressed from efficacy in the molding of the disciplines and policies by which we live. Economic theory follows Descartes in treating animals only as resources for human use, with their value determined in the marketplace. Until very recently, the notion of animal rights was not taken seriously. Meanwhile, the actual treatment of animals in factory farming expresses their economic exploitation with the perfect indifference to their feelings for which Descartes called. Massive experimentation on animals for trivial human purposes remains common. The idea that the rights of animals might significantly impinge upon people's freedom to do as they please has not yet gained significant headway against the power of Descartes' vision. The church, furthermore, has given virtually no leadership in opposing the implications of Descartes' position, for it has internalized it too thoroughly.

Through the work of German idealism, Descartes' dualism of mind and matter has become the dualism of history and nature. The results of this formulation include those already discussed, but it extends the nature that is subordinated, intentionally or unintentionally, to include many human beings as well. An obvious instance is the destruction of aboriginal Indian peoples along with the destruction of the forests in the Amazon basin. These peoples belong to nature rather than to history. Indeed, in much planning for Third World development the goal is urban-industrial growth. The subsistence farming of tribal people does not count in the measurement of economic activity, and policies are planned to displace this traditional life in a natural environment by a historically oriented one. The cost to tribal peoples and peasant villagers has been enormous.

The perception of nature and its relation to human beings has also been affected by Descartes' understanding of substance. Each thing is seen as essentially self-contained, being related to others only incidentally. The destruction of one entity is just that: one does not expect its loss to affect other things. Hence, for centuries nature could be exploited for immediate economic gain with little concern for other consequences. The connection between deforestation and flooding, for example, was largely ignored, and it fell outside economic calculations. Even today people are reluctant to acknowledge that the acid rain that is killing so many lakes and inhibiting the growth of so much vegetation is the result of industry hundreds of miles away. To point out the costly consequences of immediately profitable activities is still felt as an intrusion upon the proper freedom of economic enterprise.

This practical insensitivity to the interconnections among things is accompanied by the compartmentalization of knowledge. This is far removed from the intentions of the Enlightenment. The hope then was that one science would explain the whole of nature. The separation of the human sciences from natural science expresses the dualism of the Enlightenment as well as the accompanying insensitivity to the connection between them. But the further compartmentalization within each is an unintended result of substantialist thinking.

This thinking implies that any segment of the whole can be studied independently. Thus, any definable subject matter justifies a separate science. And each science develops methods suitable for studying its subject matter in greater and greater detail. Questions that cannot be answered within the compass of any one science are usually ignored. Otherwise they are treated by an interdisciplinary team, each of whose members applies the relevant knowledge of her or his discipline. Unfortunately, most of the most urgent questions we now confront in our quest for justice and peace are not subject to treatment by any existing discipline or combination of disciplines. This applies as much to the theological disciplines as to others, for the ideals of scholarship envisioned by the Enlightenment have been fully internalized in the church.

9. *The Global Context of Christian Identity Today*

Although it is important to our understanding of ourselves to confront the ways we have been both lifted and damned by Enlightenment individualism and dualism, it is equally important to understand the ecosociopolitical context within which we now seek to be faithful. Because an identity created by Israel's history as appropriated through Jesus Christ means accepting the whole world as the object of God's concern, our context must be global. In any case, the growing interconnectedness of all aspects of the biosphere and human involvement in it necessitates recognizing the importance of the global context to Christian self-understanding. In this sense all Christian theology today should be global theology.[16]

The single most conspicuous characteristic of the present world situation is the threat of nuclear holocaust. We know that nuclear armaments exist, such that the use of even a portion of them would lead to a nuclear winter and the end of life at least in the Northern Hemisphere. Meanwhile, the relationship between the two most heavily armed nations is deteriorating, and the arms race is escalating. At the same time, more

---

[16] Cf. Tissa Balasuriya, *The Eucharist and Human Liberation* (Mary Knoll, NY: Orbis, 1979).

and more nations are acquiring nuclear capability, and so the likelihood of a final holocaust is increasing.

The threat of nuclear war arises chiefly in relations between the First and Second Worlds, and there is a danger that it might distract attention from the already desperate condition of many Third and Fourth World countries. It is small comfort to desperately poor persons on the brink of starvation and social disintegration to hear that preventing nuclear war is the first priority. Death for them is a present reality, a common experience. Thus, although we are aware of the nuclear threat as the single most dangerous feature of the global situation today, we in the North American churches must constantly remind ourselves of the evils that the avoidance of a nuclear war will not solve: the gross imbalance of political, economic, and military power that exists between the First and Second Worlds, on the one side, and the Third and Fourth Worlds, on the other. The continuation and magnification of that unjust situation is currently one of the most salient aspects of the global context.

The problem of injustice is, of course, not only between nations. There is also gross injustice and suffering within nations, both rich and poor. The problem, from the perspective of North American Christians, is complicated because the policies recommended by our own government for the development of the lesser developed nations are implemented more often than not with the assistance of authoritarian regimes supported by military power. Those concerned for freedom and economic justice for the poor are usually silenced. Therefore, in addition to the injustice in the balance between nations, there emerges the important issue of human rights within nations.

But the problems in many nations are not only those of injustice. Alongside the oppression and exploitation of the poor by the rich there are the collapse of ancient cultural traditions and struggles among ethnic groups. In some instances effective government control is barely possible. Many nations exist in a state of perpetual violence between economic classes, ethnic groups, or other political divisions.

The international economic system is also precarious. Again, its injustices contribute to its instability, but there are other factors. Debtor nations may simply be unable to make payments. Bankruptcies of major financial institutions might follow. The whole system of international credits could collapse. The process of industrialization for which the Third World has made such great sacrifices could be reversed. The breakdown of international trade could lead not only to overwhelming unemployment but also to mass starvation in food-deficient countries. Violence within nations and wars among them would almost certainly increase.

Population growth, combined with schemes of rapid development, frequently puts pressure on the environment as well. In much of the tropical world, the firewood needed for cooking has become extremely costly because it must be brought from great distances. Meanwhile, deforestation leads to soil erosion and destructive floods. As population grows, the loss of soil is aggravated by overgrazing and by farming of marginal lands. There is less and less fertile land and less and less wood to meet the basic necessities of more and more people. The importation of oil and fertilizer, together with rapid industrialization, introduces additional imbalances in the environment.

Pressure on the environment is very much present in the First and Second Worlds. As Jonathan Schell has indicated, for a long time nature was seen as a habitat of dangerous forces by which human beings could easily be victimized and suffer irreparable loss.[17] After the rise of science and the Industrial Revolution, that situation has completely changed. Today, nature is fragile and stands before humanity as the victim. It may be the victim of either near instantaneous nuclear destruction or the degradation brought on by pollution, contamination, and ruthless exploitation by expanding industrial nations. For example, soil losses in the United States are making it less capable of meeting food deficits elsewhere. Agriculture and industry are polluting the water supply, leading to ever greater concentrations of toxic substances in the drinking water of major cities. In addition, the widespread use of chemical fertilizers and pesticides, as well as the dumping of industrial waste into rivers, is reducing the ocean's capacity to support life. Industrial wastes and automobile emissions are eroding the ozone layer, which protects us from dangerous solar radiation, and are increasing the carbon dioxide content of the atmosphere. This, in turn, is probably raising the temperature of the planet so as to threaten the arctic ice caps.

Developments in industrialized and less industrialized nations alike are destroying the habitats of many species of plants and animals. Tens of thousands of these will become extinct by the end of this century. In these and other ways, the global ecosystem is being simplified, and there is no way of foreseeing the consequences of this simplification.

How does our own nation appear in global perspective? On the one hand, it counterbalances the imperial ambitions of the Soviet Union, and thereby makes it possible for some nations to govern their own affairs who might otherwise come under Soviet domination. It maintains within its own borders a remarkable level of civil freedom. It defends other First World nations with similar policies and gives support to freedom elsewhere as well.

On the other hand, in the pursuit of these policies, the United States constitutes no less a nuclear threat to the whole globe than does the Soviet Union. Furthermore, it supports many oppressive military regimes

[17] Jonathan Schell, *The Fate of the Earth* (New York: Alfred Knopf, 1982).

as long as they share its opposition to the Soviet Union, and it encourages their suppression of freedom when it fears that those who seek freedom might not continue their alliance with the United States. In addition, the type of economic development the United States encourages, especially the investment of North American capital, requires that the host countries ensure both freedom from labor disruption and continued low wages. In this way, the policy of the United States adds to the widespread misery that accompanies industrial growth.

We must also ask what the global situation means for internal developments in the United States. If present trends are projected into the future, the struggle for continuing economic growth will be the first priority. This will mean the accelerating erosion of those elements in the national life that inhibit such growth—what economists call *rigidities*. These include the power of labor unions to force up wages in some industries. Industry, therefore, will continue to move from highly unionized areas of the country to those where unions are less well established. Multinational corporations will move much of their labor-intensive heavy industry out of the United States to other countries where labor is cheaper and more tightly controlled by authoritarian governments. This in turn will intensify the need for scientific research for high technology production so as to develop a new economic basis here.

Second only to economic growth will be the aim to be militarily superior to all rivals. This is costly and competes with the production of consumer goods. The desire for high military expenditures intensifies the pressure to increase rapidly the gross national product, so that industry can supply both "guns and butter."

To avoid restricting growth, the government will encourage both nuclear energy and the burning of fossil fuels. Because the risks of the former are well known and because the latter acidifies water and soil over vast regions, there inevitably will be protests. But procedures will be devised to limit and override them. That the atmospheric buildup of carbon dioxide from burning fossil fuels will raise global temperatures, melt the polar ice caps, flood some coastal regions, and alter agricultural patterns will simply be accepted and adjusted to as an inevitable concomitant of industrial growth. Also, for the sake of growth there will be pressure on all those governmental programs that divert resources from industrial expansion to human welfare: social security, unemployment insurance, public education, medical services for the poor, child support, environmental protection, and so forth.

The United States' churches will have to consider their life and mission in terms of these social, economic, and political prospects. They cannot be indifferent to the threat of nuclear catastrophe, nor simply view the United States' nuclear armaments as instruments of its foreign policy. They cannot ignore the present hunger of hundreds of millions of fellow human beings nor expect that the problems of feeding the world will lessen in decades ahead. They cannot ignore the price we are exacting from our children for the sake of our own prosperity or the threat to the planet's ability to provide for human habitat, which is inherent in present North American economic policies. The churches must be concerned about the loss of human freedom to which the government of the United States is making significant contributions.

10. *The Need for Images of the Church*

Every community whose identity consists of its shared history has some conscious or unconscious view of what it has been. This picture is likely to be self-congratulatory. Israel was remarkable in its ability to depict its own history realistically, giving an honest account of the sins of its heroes and of its collective failures. Christians have yielded more often than Jews to the temptation to exalt the greatness of their historical achievements, but this has been checked by the scriptures and the awareness of the need for repentance.

To have an identity molded by shared history also has normative implications. The communiy should now live and act in accordance with that identity. What this means is, of course, always debatable. For example, is the proper role of the United States, as a nation founded on revolution, to support movements of liberation around the world? Or, as a nation grown prosperous through the free market, should it support governments that suppress revolutionary movements in the name of maintaining order and supporting global systems of free enterprise? This question is discussed, to be sure, chiefly in terms of American "interests." But American interests cannot be determined apart from American identity. Are we a people dedicated to liberty and justice for all, or are we the defenders of the free world? Americans live consciously or unconsciously according to some such images of who they are.

The same is true for Christians. Precisely because Christian identity is more freely chosen and more easily denied, the images through which it is expressed are more important. To participate in a community that lives through and from shared memories is to have normative images of what that community truly is, that is, what it means today to live from those memories. For some Christians at some times the important images have been read as the victorious extension of the church and the blessing of its widening rule. The meaning of this history for those times has been that the church should complete the work of conquering all for Christ. We share in the current widespread criticism of that reading of the past, and we reject the images that followed from it. For other Christians at other times, the history of the institutional church has appeared as one of faithlessness to the teachings of Jesus which can be found, cherished, and obeyed only in obscure corners or small conventicles. This has led to images of the holy or sanctified church over and against the institutional one. We reject that image as well, believing that it too is based on a false reading of Christian history. We do not see holy conventicles within a fallen church but, rather, a mixture of sin and virtue in both.

Images of what the church truly is and should be cannot be simply projected from what the church has been. The church, like every human community, has always included both good and evil. But in living from the history of God's working with her people of Israel and the church, we discern elements of faithfulness and project from those into the present scene. The resulting images show what faithfulness means today in light of what it has meant in the past.

Pictures of the church portraying ideals disconnected from reality are not the sort of images we need. For example, a picture of the church as a harmonious fellowship of totally dedicated Christians is too remote from the actual church to be of much use. On the other hand, pictures of the church that aim simply at descriptive accuracy, though useful in their own way, are not the normative images by which the church lives. This chapter has tried to remain generally descriptive in this sense, but it is time now to move beyond such description to images of what the church would be today were it truly faithful—that is, what the church should be. To live by some such images is part of the church's identity. It matters greatly from which images it lives, even though the actuality of the church will always fall short of them. The next chapter offers images that are important to us, that many Christians share, and that we believe to be appropriate for the whole church today.

Chapter III

The Practice of the Christian Community:
Guiding Images for the Church of the Future

The church is the community which keeps alive the memory of Jesus Christ in the world. In the previous chapter, we have tried to give some account of the way in which that identity is shaped, even transformed, as the memory of Jesus Christ is recollected in the context of concrete world-historical situations. The transformation of the memory of Jesus Christ is often a distortion, to be sure, and we have alluded to the distortions which have become part of the problematic identity of the church. These distortions are very much a part of what the church is, and it is important that those distorted memories be subjected to fresh criticism in each new historical context. That process of criticism has developed during recent years, and because of it, the distortions have not been total defacements, nor have they eroded completely the possibility of the church's recovering a more authentic self-understanding in our time.

We have also sketched some salient features of our present world-historical situation. In our view, each of these features is crucial to our understanding of the world as it really is. As such, they form the context for any new attempt at developing a fresh Christian self-understanding which might yield a more authentic Christian practice here and now. Christian identity is no abstract or formal concept. Christian identity is forged by the living practice of Christians in their world. In light of this, we shall not have completed our theological understanding of the ministry of the church until we project toward the future some images by which its living practice can be guided. In what follows we offer a number of such images. They are instruments of hope, and like all hope they flow from a fresh reconsideration of who we are and from whence we have come. They represent our hope for the church in the real world as we see it.

No single set of images of the church can be judged to be final or complete, and we make no such claim for those we project here. What we do claim is that these images are faithful to the church's memory of Jesus Christ, and that they do indeed provide important base points for Christian reflection on practice now.

1. *The Church as a Human Community*

Everything we have said to this point suggests the humanness of the church in one sense. The church is finite, fallible, and sinful. As such, it is one human institution among others. However, the humanness of church institutions is not to be seen simply as a problem or a limitation. On the contrary, the primary theological understanding of human institutions is that they are among the crowning creative-redemptive achievements of God. Institutions represent the attempt of human communities to preserve and to protect what they value and to achieve the purposes which they envision for themselves as a community. They are the cultural expressions of human ideals for communities. Therefore, when we refer to the church as a human community, we mean those institutions which have organized to preserve the memory of Jesus Christ and to project the vision of what it is to be faithful to that memory as a living community.

The character of the church as a human community means that members of the church are bound together in ways that transcend their own autonomy. As in other human communities, they are united with one another without violating their individuality. As Paul Tillich has shown, the relationship between individuality and participation in community is such that one can become a true individual only through participation, and one can authentically participate only as one's individuality is given expression in the community.[1] When a human community embraces these polarities in balance, it can be said to be a *humanizing* community.

When we refer to the church as a human community, we refer to the full participation of the church in the humanizing work of God in the world which gives shape to human possibilities and hopes. The question then becomes, how is that humanizing work to be imagined? Here Karl Barth's discussion of the basic forms of human community can be helpful. His conception of community is grounded in the notion of the self as social. There is no such thing as an isolated human being; there are only co-human beings, for life not shared in community is not human. In a beautiful and freewheeling commentary on Genesis 2, Barth places co-humanity in the act of creation itself. He describes the rhythm of creation in which God begins by creating something and then approving of that work. This rhythm is maintained until the man is created. Then for the first time, God looks at the work and says that it is not good. That is, it is incomplete; so God creates woman. When both man and woman were created, the humanity of creation was called good. God created human beings with each other so that they might, by

---

[1] Paul Tillich, *Systematic Theology*, vol. 2 (Chicago: University of Chicago Press, 1957), pp. 65–66.

grace, aspire to be for one another. The primal act of creation was completed in human community. Being human is being in community.

Barth later outlines the four aspects of the basic form of human community. The first he calls *eye-to-eye relationships*. If people are to be with one another in community, each one must see and recognize the uniqueness of each of the others. Otherwise, they may be "around" but not with one another. To be able to say, "I know you by name, I know you by sight," is the first level of humanization in community. This also includes the willingness not to hide from one another.

The second level is one of mutual speech and hearing. Communication is constitutive of community, or being together. I cannot know who I am unless I hear from you about who I am, and you cannot know who I am unless I tell you. The development of the self is a social phenomenon that requires your speaking to me about my origins and my place in society and my integrating those words in my own way and projecting myself beyond the previous boundaries set for me by the social world. If we are to be "in communion" at any deeper level than the mutual dependence of individual selfhood, then speech and hearing must take on greater importance. Not only does the community need to protect my right to speak, but it also has the right to hear what I have to say. I have the obligation to address the community with genuine and significant speech, and thus to participate actively in the growth of community.

The third level to which Barth refers is mutual assistance. This is a broad-ranging claim upon us; so broad, in fact, that in Christian terms, the need of the neighbor becomes the form of the command of God to act. It is not as if one has a program of reform. Instead, armed with sensitivity to human need, one opens oneself to assist when a need is discovered. And equally important, one is ready to receive graciously when one is in need. The key here again is mutuality, and it requires the willingness to become an opportunity for another's obedience as well as the readiness to assist another.

The fourth level has to do with the attitudinal stance toward community life. Sensitive to the human tendency to become too serious and moralistic, Barth insists that such attitudes deny humanity. Being together can become a network of duties that are fulfilled grudgingly and purely for the sake of meeting survival needs. But communities should be characterized by joy and gladness, not by drudgery. Each comes to the other for the other's sake as well as one's own, and in coming together, each recognizes that all are becoming themselves and what they hope to be. In genuine giving and receiving, what all hope for—human fulfillment and community—becomes a reality. The joy of knowing that one is received by others and that they receive one gladly enables one to give, knowing that one's gifts will be received in the same joyful mood. Each trusts the other, knowing that the other is trustworthy and at the same time reciprocates that trust. No one is alone and none will be left alone. Each cares and each is cared for. Such a life together creates a community of perpetual celebration in which all abandon their inhibitions and exult in the promise and possibility made known through being with one another.[2]

2. The Church as a Caring Community

Barth's description of the basic form of humanity might be characterized as a caring community. To be sure, in every human community there is mutual care. But the Christian church elevates this to a primary image, according to which the community is marked by mutual love and structures itself so as to render this love effective in the ministry of each to the other members.

The church is, therefore, not simply a community of caring people, but a community dedicated to mutual caring and ordering its life to that end. It devises systems to ensure that word of special needs and crises within the community reaches those best able to respond, and it prepares the community members to make the appropriate responses.

The task of caring for one another has become more difficult in our pluralistic, mobile society. Unlike the parish in a region in which most people belong to a single church, the members of North American congregations may have few contacts with one another in their work and neighborhoods. What was once spontaneous can now be achieved only by intentional planning and organizing.

But the needs for mutual care have not declined. Indeed, we have already noted that our post-Enlightenment society has encouraged us to think of ourselves as autonomous individuals. The result has been to heighten the need for sustaining relationships. Loneliness and alienation are characteristics of our society that intensify in times of crisis. The functions once performed by neighbors are no longer fulfilled at all unless the church as caring community finds ways to respond.

Because the community cares for persons as persons and for families as families, there is no type of need to which it should not respond. Physical needs, economic needs, recreational needs, emotional needs, social needs, and educational needs all are important, and ideally the church is sensitive to all of them. But in dealing with many of these needs, other institutions will play a larger role than the church will. Given the limits of its resources, the church must give special attention to the needs to which other institutions expect the church to offer the primary ministry: the need to worship, to meditate, and to pray; the

[2] Karl Barth, *Church Dogmatics*, vol. 3, pt. 2, trans. Harold Krupf et al. (Edinburgh: T. & T. Clark, 1960), pp. 222ff.

need for meaning in life's major transitions and crises; and the need for guidance in determining convictions, commitments, and vision.

The principle means by which the church addresses those needs is through congregational worship including the sacraments. By this means, members learn not only to worship together but also to meditate and pray. Baptism, confirmation (or the dedication of infants and joining the church), marriage, and funerals give meaning to life's transitions and crises, and the sermon is directed particularly to forming convictions, commitments, and vision. So central to church life is worship that we shall return to it when considering the church as a worshiping community—our concluding image.

For the Christian community, prayer is the deepest and most pervasive expression of care. The church, as a community of care, will inevitably be a community of prayer as well. It is mainly in worship that Christians learn the meaning and nature of prayer. But prayer is not simply the life of the gathered community in worship. The whole of the Christian life is to be a life of prayer. Prayer is life lived before God, in God, with God, and in the awareness of God's spirit, creatively and redemptively present within the believer. According to Paul, Christians are to pray without ceasing. To do so is to live open to God, trusting her, attentive to her call, responsive to her prompting, rejoicing in her love, and therefore seeing and loving all other creatures with her—especially those who belong to the household of faith. Though prayer is much more than speaking, it is true that from time to time the prayerful life comes naturally to speech. The speech of prayer is addressed to God in response to the spirit. Its content is determined by the Christian's perception of what appears to be most urgent for the outworking of God's love, whether through the one who prays or through other agents of God's activity.

The speech of prayer does not simply happen but most often becomes habitual through disciplined practice. Many Christians find it helpful to set aside special times, in addition to corporate worship, in order to practice disciplines that promote the mindfulness of God's presence in the midst of other activities and that encourage changing from habits of personal willfulness into habits of sensitive caring for one another.

3. The Church as an Evangelistic Community

Although the image of a caring community differentiates the church from many other human communities, it does not carry us far into its distinctive identity, the subject of Chapter I. The church is a caring, human community that lives by and from a particular history, a history within which there are illumining events—most decisively the event of Jesus Christ. The church is the community that tells this story and, through song and painting as well as through reading and interpreting scripture, witnesses this revelation.

The telling of this story is also the greatest expression of caring. Those who know the story's healing and directive power want others to know it too. Those who are aware of how easily the story is misrepresented and distorted—sometimes into a means of self-justification—want to ensure that it can be heard rightly. Those who see new implications in the story for the present life of the community want to bring these out for critical discussion.

The church as a whole is particularly concerned that the community's children and youth find in the church's story their own story and are thereby engrafted into the ongoing movement that is Christianity. Much of the energy of many congregations goes, therefore, into the evangelization of the next generation. The Christian movement can continue only by converting successive generations to identify with it.

But Christian communities are not content to share the story only internally. Christians believe that there are many outside the community of faith whose lives are confused by not having a revelatory story to provide them with adequate identity. There are many who idolatrously give themselves to causes and goods that are unworthy of devotion. There are many who seek to save themselves through techniques that inevitably fail. There are many who live without hope. There are many who try to understand all things around a center hardly larger than themselves when in truth nothing is rightly understood except in the light of God's universality. The story by which Christians live is one that can bring salvation to many.

Just because the story has such power, the church must be especially careful that it not be distorted in its public telling. Too often it is presented in such a way as not to overcome idolatry but to propose a new idolatry. Too often it is prevented, in truncated telling, from speaking of universal grace and is instead associated with efforts at self-salvation that will not work. Too often the "hope" it offers is so incredible and so bound up with punitive legalism that the sensitive hearer is confirmed in despair. Too often God is presented as the sanction of values and procedures that express a very narrow perspective, instead of as the one who makes relative all creaturely perspectives, including that of the story's teller. Too often the telling of this distorted story is called *evangelism*, with the result that this word has itself become almost unusable.

True evangelism is offering the good news to all who may benefit from it. It is not directed primarily toward the recruitment of members for the community, although the community rightly rejoices when some who hear the story decide to join with the community whose identity is constituted by the story. The community knows that the story's saving meaning is never understood all at once, but only bit by bit in changing circumstances, and that apart from a community sharing this story in the context of mutual concern and caring, the story's power can have only limited realization.

The passion to share the good news leads to many problems and ambiguities. At its worst it becomes a competition among rival tellers who seek to take members from one another's communities. But even when this is avoided, there remains the question of how, and even whether, the story should be told at all to those who live by other ancient, rich, and saving stories. Should Christians who learned their basic story from Jews tell it now to Jews in its Christian form? In view of centuries of Jewish heroism in preserving and continuing the Jewish story in face of Christian oppression and persecution and in view of the ready availability of the Christian story to those Jews who wish to learn it, penitence and silent listening seem a more fitting Christian stance toward Jews.

What then of Muslims, Hindus, Buddhists, and the others? Does the Christian imperative to preach the gospel apply to them, or do we respect their identity, shaped by their different histories, and remain silent? General answers are not enough. Muslims have already assimilated much of our story into their own, albeit in ways that to us seem insufficient and inaccurate. Our responsibility toward them cannot be the same as that toward those to whom our story is new. With the latter, surely it is better to share our story, while at the same time really listening to theirs.

The main concern of genuine Christian evangelism, then, is not to deny the validity of religious experience available in other great religious ways. Efforts to "prove" that the Christian story is "superior" to other stories simply are not appropriate. The concern of the evangelistic community will always be that the story that we know to be true is told in such a way as to indicate its great potential for helping people to recognize and understand the creative-redemptive work of God in the world. That story is most persuasively conveyed by the authentic life of a Christian community whose practice gives evidence that its story is good news, not merely for itself, but for the whole world.

4. The Church for the World

The good news of the Christian story is that God's activity has become manifest in this world here and now. It was for the love of this world that God sent her son to save it. For that reason, the church, whose central memory is that of Jesus Christ's obedience, can never be simply *in* the world. Affirming this memory of Jesus Christ, the church as church is *for* the world.

We mentioned in Chapter II Dorothee Soelle speaks of the Christian commitment to "the indivisible salvation of the whole world." In Section 3 of this chapter, we noted the important role of preaching the gospel—telling the story—in seeking that indivisible salvation. But commitment to the world cannot be expressed only as the rescue of some individuals from despair and idolatry. Nor can it be expressed simply as the salvation of human beings, their institutions, and their culture. The world is a whole, and the church exists in that whole. It is not estranged from the world. Its members feel at home here, knowing that they have been given their place by the grace of the one who gives them everything they have. Without this place, there is no possibility for the beginning of community or its growth or sustenance. Our place, then, is our place only in the sense that we are part of it. The world, living and nonliving, is a mutually sustaining web of interdependence. Human beings are, as Aldo Leopold put it, a part of the life pyramid, the complex, dynamic, and vital ongoing system in which each part is integral to the whole and in which the good of each part derives from and participates in the good of the whole.

At this point the relationship between creation and covenant becomes important. The biblical notion of creation is grounded in the covenant by which the community came into being, but at the same time the biblical accounts make clear that covenant is for the sake of the whole creation. Thus the scope of the covenant is defined by the accounts of creation, and the wider meaning of God's covenant with Abraham is clear only when it is referred to the covenant with Noah. The children of Abraham become Abraham's children precisely because they are to be the people of the rainbow, those who are party to God's covenant for the whole earth. Therefore, it is not as if the rest of the world is at the disposal of humanity simply to be its place. On the contrary, one might say that human beings are at the disposal of God for the world. Those who are in the image of God are in the image of one who loves the whole world. Human dominion over the earth, which is itself a gift, must be a dominion analogous to the dominion of God over the earth—a rule which is for the sake of those who are ruled. It must be a rule that is loving, caring, and creative—one that bestows upon the world a gift of life with the hope of fulfillment.

Although it is true that only human beings participate in the *imago dei*, this does not imply that only human life is important. Humans live in a place with other creatures, all of whom are valued by God. God has pronounced them all good. The goodness of creation for God lies precisely in the beauty of its interrelationships whereby the being of each creature is constituted by its being with all the rest. It is this vision for which the prophets were groping as they spoke of wolves lying down with lambs and the pounding of swords into plowshares and of spears into pruning hooks. The dream of the peaceable kingdom is a vision of

God's relationship to the whole world, and that relationship is a redemptive and ecological connection. That is why the writer of Colossians can speak of Christ as all in all, everything for everything; and this is what Paul pointed to when he told the Romans of the eager longing and straining of the whole cosmos toward the salvation of the people of Christ, the one in whom all things were made and in whom all things now find their hope. Jesus Christ is the harbinger of God's ecological community, and the sign of that community is the church.

Unfortunately, this biblical and Christian vision of the world as the place of human life has been distorted, especially in the Enlightenment, into a mechanistic and materialistic world view from which only human minds are exempted. The world for which the church has concern has thus been shrunk to the human world. Soelle, when she speaks of the indivisible salvation of the whole world, does not seem to notice that human beings cannot be saved apart from the salvation of other living creatures, of soil and water and air. Humanity is indivisibly bound up with its place. Where this intimate relatedness is neglected, human suffering is increased, the prospects for future generations grow dim, and our fellow creatures are destroyed.

Awareness of the destructive consequences of human actions for the environment has now become commonplace and has led to a more careful reading of the Bible. Israel recognized that its covenant with God required replenishment of the earth as well as justice among human beings and that these are interconnected. True, Israel knew humanity as the rightful lord of creation, but in Jewish understanding the lord rules in the service of the ruled. Only when this lordship was separated from this Jewish understanding could it become a justification for ruthless exploitation of the earth. This "anthropocentric fallacy" in fact reversed the entire notion of stewardship so central to Jewish theology. This has been clearly demonstrated by Odil Steck in his *World and Environment*.[3] In Paul's vision the whole creation will share in the final salvation;[4] there is no dualism of the human and natural worlds.

5. *The Church for the Poor*

The church is a community for the whole world, human and non-human, but along with this note of universality, the Bible continually strikes a note of particularity. For the service of the world, God chose Israel, and among the people of Israel, God chose individuals to be their leaders and prophets. Finally, God chose Jesus. But even within Israel, God concentrated on the poor, and it is these same poor who were the

---

[3] Odil Hannes Steck, *World and Environment* (Nashville: Abingdon Press, 1980).
[4] Romans 8:18–23.

objects of Jesus' special concern as well. This is illustrated by a series of events reported by Luke. In his account of Jesus' ministry, Luke put these events into a sequence. The first was a baptism at which the title "Son of God" was given to Jesus and in which the descent of the Spirit upon Jesus was described.

The second event was the temptation in the wilderness. Here, most New Testament commentators have agreed that from the mouth of Satan came popular notions of messiahship that were in vogue at the time. Satan offered a series of proposals that Jesus spurned with aphorisms from the scriptures. The fact that the dialogue between Jesus and Satan was really about the nature of messiahship indicates that Luke considered the wilderness period to be a time not only of temptation but also of growing clarity for Jesus about the direction of his own ministry. It is not surprising, then, to discover that Luke placed Jesus in an active teaching role as soon as he returned from the wilderness.

The third event in the sequence takes on special importance because it was Jesus' first return to Nazareth after his wilderness experience. His fame had been growing, and the people were curious about the young and famous rabbi who had given some sparkle to Nazareth's reputation. Moreover, it is reasonable to assume that Luke saw this foray into Nazareth to be crucial to setting the tone for Jesus' ministry.

When Jesus appeared in a synagogue, Luke reported that he was handed a scroll to read and that he chose a familiar passage from Isaiah: "The spirit of the Lord is on me because he has anointed me to preach good news to the poor and the recovery of sight to the blind, release to the captives and freedom to the oppressed, to proclaim the acceptable year of the Lord" (Luke 4:18). Luke then wrote that as the eyes of all were fixed on him, Jesus announced that what they had heard was fulfilled before them.

This passage clearly has the force of a revolutionary concept of messiahship. It picks up aspects of the most important revolutionary social innovation in Jewish history, the Year of Jubilee, the acceptable year of the Lord. The legislation establishing the celebration over fifty years included a provision for canceling debts, reassigning land to the dispossessed, freeing slaves and servants, and freeing the land for itself and for nonhuman creatures.

When one understands the cultural context within which this reading took place, it is not surprising that a short time later, a group of the good citizens of Nazareth tried to push Jesus off the cliff. Jesus had asserted the primacy of concern for the poor in God's creative relationship to the world. This was said in a cultural milieu based on the theological understanding that it was the rich who were the objects of God's special favor. The alliance of religiousness and riches was, of course, not a new theological position. At least as early as Job, the notion that the faithful would be prospered by God was prominent. In Job's case, his accusers' main charge was that because he no longer prospered, he must have offended God. It was evident to them that poverty and misfortune accompanied unfaith, whereas the faithful always were rewarded with good fortune.

Although the Book of Job was written as a protest against this idea, and much of the prophetic tradition sided theologically with the poor, the view of Job's friends dominated the religiously based culture into which Jesus was born. Despite their position as a colonized people, many Jews of Jesus' time, like many Christians today, made the same association of riches and religiousness, so much so that to be poor was almost by definition to be a sinner. The poor could not count among the truly religious. This convenient theological perspective also undergirded the political alliance of the Sadducees and Pharisees which spearheaded the religious opposition to Jesus.

What Jesus said at Nazareth, then, turned all of this on its head. Not only were the poor to be included in the covenant people, they were the object of God's special concern. God is God for the poor, and the people of God are the people for the poor—living, working, and moving on their behalf.

In a recent book, Luise Schottroff suggests that even this does not go far enough. Not only was Jesus *for* the poor in his ministry, he called together a community that *was* poor. In other words, the community of the people of God was initiated as a community of the poor. It may have been part of a general movement referred to in some of the literature as "the piety of the poor," which was a grass roots Jewish protest of the alliance between riches and religiousness that characterized the official leadership.[5]

In light of Jesus' teaching and practice, it was riches that became the problem for the followers. Poverty needed no justification, but wealth did. Even when the church settled down to wealth and power after the Constantinian establishment, those who wanted to be fully religious took vows of poverty. The Reformers continued the tradition of suspicion of wealth. But gradually, in recent times, the association of poverty with sin recurred. The wealthy became complacent. Even their charity toward the poor was marked by condescension and paternalism, as the giving was often a way of keeping the poor at a distance.

We are trying now to renew our understanding of the church for the poor. The challenge is profound. As Gustavo Gutierrez has said, "The poor today, rather than being regarded as merely a 'problem for the

[5] See Luise Schottroff and Wolfgang Stegemann, *Jesus von Nazareth: Hoffnung der Armen* (Stuttgart: Kohlhammen, 1978). See also Werner G. Kummel, *Introduction to the New Testament*, trans. Howard C. Kee (New York: Abingdon Press, 1973), p. 139.

church,' raise the question of what 'being the church' really means."[6]

First, it means being with the poor. The church will include the poor within it. Where it exists apart from the poor, this fact alone will be a matter of great concern. For the community of God's people, those who are rich will be greatly disturbed at their separation from the poor, and this concern will be manifested in a persistent and genuine outreach for community with the poor.

Second, if the church is for the poor, it will be for the poor even at the risk of itself. It will be ready to sacrifice itself for the poor, and it will take whatever risks are required to ensure that there is good news to proclaim to the poor—genuine good news that there is new life and new hope.

Third, if the church is for the poor, the church will listen to them. It will not dismiss their ideas because they lack advanced formal education. It will realize that such education, together with our inherited theologies, can block perceptions as well as deepen them. The rich and the educated have much to preserve and defend: in particular their property and their status. The poor have nothing. They may be consumed by an envy that is as distorting as defense is, but they can also be free, as the rich never are, to see things as they are.

The concern of the church for the poor will be evident only when the poor know that the church sees them, the poor, as the vanguard of the Year of Jubilee. The signs of the year of the Lord will be *their* freedom, *their* hope, and *their* new life. In short, the progress of the poor out of oppression and captivity is the sign of the fiftieth new year and a new kingdom. All other progress is, as Bloch has put it, "darkly progressive."[7]

In this way not only will the church be the hope for the poor, but the poor are the givers of hope for the church. As Dumas has put it, the two faces of Christ, the poor and the church, cannot remain alienated and expect to be whole. It is only when they are together, fully with each other and for each other, that the faces of Christ are united and the body of Christ really becomes one.[8]

6. The Church for All Peoples

We have used the term *poor* to speak of those with whom God particularly identifies. The term refers in the first instance to those who lack adequate economic goods. In biblical language the poor are virtually

[6] Gustavo Gutierrez, "The Poor in the Church," quoted in Julio de Santa Ana, *Toward a Church of the Poor* (Mary Knoll, 1981), p. 122.

[7] Ernst Block, *A Philosophy of the Future*, trans. John Cumming (New York: Herder and Herder, 1970), p. 113.

[8] Bernard Dumas, *The Two Alienated Faces of the One Church*, referred to in Santa Ana, op. cit., p. 99.

identical with the oppressed, and today, in the United States also, the connection is very close. Those who are oppressed because of race, for example, are for the most part kept poor, so that the church for the poor will inevitably be at the same time the church for ethnic minorities, especially blacks, native Americans, and latinos. The long history of exploitation, expropriation, and discrimination against these peoples complicates what has been said about the church for the poor.

Nevertheless, it is important to recognize that racism has dimensions that are not reducible to economics. Many were made poor and are kept poor even today because of their race, and even those members of the "colored" races who do escape from poverty often encounter rejection in white society, including the white churches in the United States. Until very recently, explicitly racist laws abounded on the statute books. Racist mores are far from dead.

It was above all blacks who forced upon the American consciousness the depth and evil of racism. Their history was not one merely of poverty but also of being hunted and enslaved in Africa, brought to this country in chains, bought and sold like animals, denied rights to family, and kept ignorant by law. When slavery was finally abolished, it was followed by legal segregation, inferior schools, and systems of economic exploitation, many explicitly racist. And all of this was done to blacks by whites, most of whom called themselves Christians; it was justified by a white Christian society, and it was often sanctified by white Christian churches. Blacks now ask white Christians to reexamine the very nature of a "Christianity" that for centuries could sanction this systematic racist exploitation. Black theologians have challenged the whites' claim that the theology that supports such behavior can be found in the Bible. How can whites claim to worship the biblical God of the oppressed when they have not rejected the forms of biblical interpretation and worship that have accompanied the radical dehumanization of blacks?

Although blacks have been the most articulate critics of the white churches, other nonwhite groups in this country have similar horror stories. Worst of all is the story of the white Americans' treatment of native Americans. They would no doubt have been enslaved had they not shown a preference for death. The attitude of white Christians to the native peoples of this region was frequently truly genocidal. Even when they were not simply slaughtered, they were pushed onto reservations in areas that whites thought they did not want. Treaties were broken whenever whites saw something more to be gained. In these ways much of the native American way of life was destroyed. Efforts to assimilate them into white culture constituted a final attack on their identity.

This history of white Christian treatment of nonwhite groups in the United States indicates that the church for all peoples cannot simply be a white church that opens its doors to people of other races. Such a church is still in danger of sanctifying white values and asking others to assimilate themselves into a church that embodies them. Christians are gradually learning that the Bible is not well understood by complacent and powerful people. When read through their eyes it is turned into a message of reassurance for individuals who have personal psychological problems. In fact, it is much more a promise of liberation directed to the powerless. At fundamental levels illiterate black slaves understood the scriptures more accurately than did their white masters or most of the famous biblical scholars of the nineteenth and twentieth centuries. A church for all peoples is a church in which not only ethnic minorities have positions of influence and power but also in which the Bible is read through eyes open to the many traditions of human suffering.

The call to be the church for all peoples is a call to community by the many separated and estranged Christian communities to begin to show the unity of the broken body of Christ. It includes the furtherance of community wherever it may be found, whether or not it is Christian, and the encouragement of community among all communities.

Not surprisingly, the World Council of Churches has done most to guide Christian thinking about a church for all peoples. Its work suggests a double form of Christian practice. For the sake of the world, the poor, and the oppressed, the church is called to realize its unity, holiness, catholicity, and apostolicity. Only in this way can it face that future to which God calls the world and be a source of hope in the present world. Only a church for all peoples can reflect adequately the mission of a global church.

But the church's unity, holiness, catholicity, and apostolicity are not made manifest by reflecting on the inner life of the church itself. God does not call the church to be the church for itself. The call is to be in union for the whole world and to reach for universal inclusiveness in its understanding of God's creative and redemptive work. The call is also to be apostolic and holy in conforming its life and ministry to those of Jesus Christ. That life and ministry were for the poor and the oppressed. But being for the oppressed, as we have seen, requires more than sympathy and relief. It requires the active envisioning with the oppressed of a global situation that will mitigate their suffering. And that vision must be set in the context of genuine care for the world, not just for the sake of those now alive or even only for future generations of humanity, but also for the sake of the world that God loves.

For these reasons, the vision of one, holy, catholic, and apostolic church is a vision of the world in which justice, participation, and sustainability mark human and nonhuman life together. It is this integration of the understanding of the church and its practice in the world that must be central to a church for all peoples.

7. The Church for Women

The poor have always been oppressed, and at least in recent times, persons have been oppressed for no other reasons than the color of their skin. But these are not the only causes of oppression. There is also gender. White males' attitudes toward women and nonwhite peoples have often been similar. Women continue to be underrepresented in higher-paying positions in society. They are still often paid less than men are even when their work is equivalent. Through much of history they have been denied property rights and have themselves been treated as property. To this day they constitute a disproportionate segment of the poorest of the world's poor. But the paramount issues for the church in relation to women are distinct from those discussed above in regard to the poor and nonwhite groups. These issues have special and peculiar importance for the church.

Whereas the poor are largely invisible to many churchgoers in Middle America, and ethnic minorities often are members of distant congregations, women make up the larger part of the membership and active participants in most local churches. These women are raising fundamental and quite distinctive questions about their role in the churches, including ethnic majority churches, and about the reasons for their age-old exclusion from leadership. Women also are articulating a new vision of the church's future. A church for women will be a church which lives into this new feminist vision and thereby into all of the images we are proposing.

The Christian church arose in a context that had long been patriarchal. The subordination of women to men has characterized all of the major historical civilizations. The church inherited from Judaism a way of thinking of deity from which feminine elements had been largely excluded. In the origins of the new movement, social conventions were strained. Jesus treated women with notable respect as persons. Women played important roles in the earliest Christian communities, and Paul saw that in Christ there is neither male nor female. The tenderness of the seeking love of God as pictured in some of Jesus' teachings suggests the motherly as much as, or more than, the fatherly as characteristic of God. Some early Christians related Jesus to the feminine Sophia rather than the masculine Logos.

But Jewish and Hellenistic patriarchal conventions quickly gained control of church practice and teaching. As the church adopted ascetic ideals, men portrayed women more and more as sources of the sexual desires they now viewed as temptations. The resulting mysogyny corrupted the church's teaching, leading to doctrines more destructive of women than were those of either the Jews or the Greeks. This evil culminated in the centuries during which hundreds of thousands, even millions, of women were murdered as witches through judicial processes sponsored by the church.

The Enlightenment world view, with its sharp dualism between the human and the natural, helped stop the witchcraft hysteria, but in its turn also further degraded women. Carolyn Merchant in *The Death of Nature* shows that because in the male imagination, women belonged to nature, the shift from an organic to a mechanistic view of nature further dehumanized them even more.[9] Of course, Enlightenment individualism also allowed exceptional women to enter the male world and eventually contributed to increasing their legal rights and suffrage. However, the church has often defended the patriarchal family against rights for women. Thus women, who provide much of the church's human and material support, find that this support is often used to keep them "in their place." The church for women, on the other hand, can only be a church that supports women in their struggle for full human freedom in the community.

The church for women cannot be ruled by men. Every office in the church must be open to women. This must not be merely a formal and technical offer. It must be an effort to hasten the day when women can be equal leaders in the church.

But simply replacing men leaders with women does not capture the full meaning of a church for women. Women distinguish between the authoritative exercise of power typical of a patriarchy and a relational power more suitable for a church for women. The authoritarian exercise of power is hierarchical and controlling. It moves in one direction. The more power is exercised from above, the less freedom remains for self-determination below. The relational exercise of power is more widely shared. It is exercised for the sake of empowerment of others. Thus the more power leaders exercise, the more powerful are the others. Also the power of the others enhances the power of the leaders. Relational power is reciprocal power. A church for women is one in which women are empowered and encouraged to exert power, but in that fashion which is mutually empowering.

The church for women will not only include women in large numbers among its leaders and govern its life with relational-reciprocal forms of power; it will also envision God's power differently. The creative-redemptive activity of God in the world, illumined above all in Jesus Christ, will be seen not to operate in an authoritarian, hierarchical pattern but in a relational, reciprocal one. God's power does not reduce our freedom, but establishes and enhances it. It empowers us to give ourselves to the service of God's creative-redemptive work. We are enabled

9 Carolyn Merchant, *The Death of Nature: Women, Ecology, and the Scientific Revolution* (San Francisco: Harper & Row, 1980).

to enhance the empowering power of God.

The church for women will not cease to be the church for men as well. It will free men as well as women from false ideas of human and divine power, from needs to subject, control, and dominate both women and nature, from the false sense of separated, isolated selfhood intensified in the Enlightenment, from estrangement from their own bodies, from an ascetic spirituality, and from the repression of natural and healthy feelings with which all this is associated. The liberation of women will be the liberation of men as well.

These are fragments of the rich vision thoughtful women hold before the church. It is profoundly revolutionary, but like most revolutions, it calls us to be what in our origins we were destined to become. It is a vision already prefigured in the New Testament, and then betrayed, as unredeemed habits of mind and social practices gained ascendancy in the church.

8. *The Church as Integrator*

The global character of the church, together with the global perspective of genuine Christian practice, has universal implications. The unity of the church is expressed in its concern for the whole world, and the mark of Christian practice is its awareness of the interconnectedness of creation and the inseparability of creation and redemption. This in turn means that the word of the church is about the whole world and to the world as a whole.

On the other hand, the paradigm governing the thought of the modern world has encouraged fragmentation. It has pictured the world as a congeries of substances or entities that exist in distinct and self-contained isolation from one another. The world view has been reflected in the isolation of persons from one another, in the alienation of groups from one another, in the separation of nature from humanity, and in the opposition of the world to God.

Because the world is seen as composed of discrete things or types of things that exist separately from one another, the study of the world has been based on isolating these discrete types of things. Physics deals with atomic and subatomic phenomena. Chemistry deals with molecules. Biology deals with cells and objects composed of them. Each of these is in turn divided into many subdisciplines with distinct subject matters and methods.

The model of discrete substances affects the methods within the sciences as well. The dominant study of an animal organism is in the laboratory. It is assumed that removing the animal from its normal habitat does not affect it in any fundamental way. One learns about its behavior in a controlled environment. To explain its behavior one operates upon its body, or injects chemical substances into it. The assumption is that as one studies the behavior of portions of its body in separation from the whole, one learns how they function within the whole.

Insofar as one seeks an integrated view of the results of these sciences, one must find the principle of explanation at the most primitive level. If the rabbit's behavior is explained by analysis into organs, organs by analysis into cells, cells by analysis into molecules, molecules by analysis into atoms, and atoms by analysis into subatomic entities, then it is finally these entities that explain the rabbit and everything else as well. But it is hard to achieve an integration in this way, for it is hard to believe that the scientific investigator is also explained by the subatomic entities. Human activity seems to require a different order of explanation. Mind must be juxtaposed to matter, the human to the natural. The closest one can come to integration is dualism.

But dualism does not work well. First the human is simply not sufficiently discontinuous from the natural for the evidence to support dualism. Second, within the natural there is much that resists this reductionism. Third, when one studies the subatomic world one cannot find the self-contained units, explanatory of themselves and of all else besides, that this reductionistic approach requires.

The evidence fits much better another model. According to this model, the world is not made up of discrete substances but of interrelated events. No event can be separated from its complex pattern of relations. The behavior of a rabbit is different according to whether it is in its natural habitat or in a laboratory. The behavior of the rabbit's organs is different according to whether they are functioning within the living body or in isolation. The cells in the organ behave differently when they are part of the organ than when they are separated. And this is true all the way down. The subatomic world is a field of events that have no reality in isolation from one another.

This ecological model can assimilate what has been learned from the reductionist model. It does not artificially separate the human from the natural. It accounts for much that the reductionistic model leaves obscure. And it fits the reality of both the subatomic world and the animal. The church can gain much in its pursuit of an integrated vision by relating to this new model of reality.

However, the church for generations has been attempting to find a modus vivendi with a fragmented world in which its claim to offer a composite vision of the whole creation and to project a relevant practice in light of that vision seems strangely out of place. In fact, recent preceptive commentators on contemporary Christianity have pointed out that beginning with the Enlightenment, the function of religion in general has been continuously narrowed from that of an ongoing center of meaning for the whole of human life, until it is now largely relegated to the private and subjective sphere of personal meaning. Worse still, religion serves often merely as a cultural form subservient to organizing centers quite distinct from it. In other words, even personal meaning is often defined primarily in relation to nonreligious institutions, and religion simply becomes a cultural adornment or a rationalization for the dominant organizing center of meaning.

At its best, the church has resisted accepting either of these roles. Its faith is in a God who is the universal creator and redeemer, who lays claims on all of life and society's institutions. In reality, of course, the church is simply one institution alongside others, and it always has been. That is not arguable. What the memory of the church resists, however, is the confinement of its concern to one aspect of life. The church has always urged on its members the understanding of each aspect of life in the perspective of faith in one God in whom all things are bound together.

We do not propose that the church today can reclaim all science and scholarship. But the church can ally itself with the movement of thought that is recovering the awareness of the interdependence and interconnectedness of all things. The church can confidently talk about an integrated vision of the world, one that is in harmony with its own memory and faith. Indeed, it is high time for the church to move toward fulfilling its proper role of helping people center their lives in their faith in God.

The question is not whether the church will take on this task—it cannot avoid it—but whether it will take seriously the problems in doing it well. It has unique resources. The impulse to integrate, ignited by faith in God, has always pushed the church toward genuine catholicity. The church also contains a wide variety of competent persons who are increasingly aware of the urgency of integrating the vision of life from the perspective of faith. At the conciliar level, evidence of this shared concern has already emerged, and there is reason to believe that this concern will continue to grow and develop.

9. *The Church as a Community of Repentance*

The call to be for the world, for the poor, for all peoples, and for women, and to project an integrated vision for the world raises great joy and expectation in the church. But it also arouses fear and trembling. The church sees painfully the contrast of its present reality with what adequate response to the call entails. It knows itself to be a community of sinners who live from the world rather than for it.

The church lives its existence in paradox. It knows that what it now is is not what by grace it is called to be. More often than not, the church lives as if injustice is tolerable and the mindless destruction of the world is permissible so long as the life of the community remains a context within which personal satisfaction of a sort is possible and the institution itself can grow in size. This is all the more satisfying if the church becomes a support institution for those for whom its members have their most immediate concerns, their families.

We have emphasized the positive aspects of such an interpersonal community in the images of the church as human community and as caring community. But to limit the vision of the church in this way is finally to engage in a refusal of the gift of God. The gift of God to the church is not only the gift of being together, but of being together with God for the sake of the whole world.

Because its own life is a refusal of the gift of God, the confession of the church has two dimensions. On the one hand, the church will be in a constant state of self-critical reflection in which it calls itself to account for its sin, its failure to live by God's call. But on the other hand, its self-criticism is not an end in itself. It is never self-condemnation. It is possible only in light of the knowledge of grace, and it is therefore followed by a movement toward renewal.

God's creative-redemptive activity in the church is experienced as the forgiveness of the past and the transformation of the present by the power of love. But the church is reminded that it is a community of sinners not only by its own inner speech and hearing, but also by criticism from outside. Since God works also in and through those who are outside the church, the word addressed to the church, even and especially by its detractors, is to be taken with utmost seriousness.

It is at this point that Marxist criticism against the churches becomes important. The charge that the churches have been, and are, obsessed with inner and private concerns to the exclusion of concern with the oppression of the poor, and that the churches have both wittingly and unwittingly resisted change and supported the status quo to the disadvantage of the poor and oppressed of the world—these charges and others have become important to the church's own self-critical understanding.

Similarly, charges from sensitive ecologists that the church's theological understanding has contributed to the development of attitudes toward nature that have resulted in an exploitive and destructive relationship of humanity to the whole of the nonhuman creation also contain a word of truth. There can be little doubt that the religiously based ideas of human dominance and disdain for this world, in favor of hope for another, have helped release the powers of destruction upon the place in which we have been given life.

In either case, the confession of the body of Christ as a community of sinners is that the speech of the church's external critics is transformed by God's grace so that our hearing is not merely the hearing of the church's enemies. What we hear again is the word of truth about ourselves, and we make that word our word to ourselves. In this way, external criticism finally becomes internal criticism.

The church must also face its share of responsibility in the development of anti-Semitism. The history of the church's relationships with the Jewish community directly challenges any claims to its being faithful to the God who calls her people to be her people when and where she will. The church, following the guidance of the Apostle Paul, needs to wrestle with the reality of God's truth as universal truth. With that reflection, all claims to exclusivity with respect to the mediation of God's truth for the world have to be modified. If the church understands its own community to be a gift from God, it can rejoice when God, relating to other communities, chooses them to be instruments of her truth about the world.

This does not mean that there can be no unique Christian witness. The church keeps alive the memory of Jesus Christ; that is the center of its life. However, the meaning of Jesus Christ is the memory of universal forgiveness. It is the affirmation of God's concern for all people. And that memory cannot be fully understood apart from God's ongoing covenant with Jews. In this sense, the Christian memory includes and affirms the memory of God's call to the Jews. Christians are the children of Abraham, and so are the Jews.

The Holocaust is an ever-present reminder of the Christian failure to remember this authentic history. It is the external evidence of Christian pride and arrogance. As such, it remains the most powerful claim for the Christian community to acknowledge God's relationship to the world in which the ongoing vitality of Judaism is part of God's relationship to her chosen people.

Black theology functions both as external and internal criticism. Black American theology is internal criticism in that it speaks from within the Christian community to the white Christian community about its failure to be what it is called to be, while at the same time it also speaks to the black community about its failure to become what it ought to be. Yet it is a special indictment of white-dominated churches in the United States for their contradiction of the call of God to be a liberating, caring community, with special attention to the oppressed blacks in the United States. White middle-class churches are the main targets of the critical comments about the duplicity of the Christian community.

In this sense, black theology is external to white Christianity. It is so alienated from white churches that it sees *them* as external to the church. Black American theology is also an internal criticism of black churches calling them into account for their failure to be this-worldly and concrete in their word to the poor and the oppressed. In both ways, it has become a source of insight for all of the churches. It has called attention to the sin of racism in American Christianity, and it has pronounced judgment upon the churches for that sin. It is a source of true judgment and also part of the church's ongoing task of developing a more adequate self-understanding.

Similarly, the liberation theologies of Latin American theologians are both *internal and external* criticism. They are external criticisms of most North Atlantic congregations for their easy alliance with a variety of unholy empires that have a long history of exploiting the poorer countries. Like black American theology, liberation theology speaks also from within the church to the church. This word, too, is often expressed as an external criticism, but it is only the failure of the First World congregations to hear the word of truth about themselves that makes it so. As the dialogue continues, this criticism must be incorporated into every congregation's own self-understanding as a true word of judgment from within about our corporate failure to be with and for the poor.

Feminist theologians, too, have been important to the church's self-critical task. Reminding the churches of the discriminatory sexism that pervades their life, governance, ordination, and theology, feminist theologians call for a confession by the churches of their sin against women and a movement toward genuine inclusiveness at all levels of the church's life and thought.

It is important to see that this dynamic of alienation, conflict, and criticism is absolutely necessary as part of the mutual speech and hearing which is the heart of the growing consciousness of Christian community. Without the speech of black American, feminist, and liberation theologians, the patterns of exclusiveness and complacency which have characterized most of the white Western European and North American churches would persist. The contradiction of what we are as the body of Christ would thus become more serious, and the circle of community narrower. Thus, speech *to* the white Western churches is part of the process of community building. And so is the hearing. If the criticism is heard as the word of truth and taken seriously, there is hope that the dynamics of mutual speech and hearing shall have brought us to a higher stage of genuine and universal community as the body of Christ.

It is, of course, too early yet to see how the conflict will be handled. What is essential, however, is that the response of white Western Christians move beyond that of fear and hostility about the words spoken against them toward the recognition that the word of judgment is true.

When the confession of the church is broadened to include the word of truth which is perceived as coming from without, so that it is part of our own word to ourselves about our sin, the community, properly chastened, stands again before the possibility of renewal and belief that it can be a community for the world. In other words, in confession hope is renewed, and that hope is that the world will be sustained and redeemed. Therefore, the church's proclamation is not only to itself as a sinful community but to the world as a sinful world. Like its self-address, the word to the world is at once promise and criticism, and the critique of the world is not a damning word, but takes the form of internal criticism from those who speak to the world from within it. It becomes a theological critique of the social and political denials of God's call. It is calling the world into account for the world's own sake.

10. *The Church as the Community of Holiness*

The church can never be self-righteous about itself. The rhythm of confession and renewal is its life. In confession, the church faces squarely the reality that it now is—a community of sin in the world of sin. But the basis for its renewal is the conviction that the church is called to become no less than the the community of holiness. By this we mean that the churches are called to be the communities in which a distinct Christian commitment is affirmed. That commitment is to be a community in which the practices of faith, hope, and love are habitual. In other words, the community of holiness is the community within which the Christian character is both nurtured and expressed by the practice of distinctly Christian virtues—faith, hope and love. This does not mean, of course, that only Christians are virtuous or that only these virtues are, or ought to be, practiced by Christians. But the virtues to which we refer when we speak of the church as the community of holiness are those practices which are central to our common memory. They are the permanent and distinctive virtues of Christian community as such.

The virtues of Christian community are human virtues. Since the church is a human community, the virtues practiced by Christians are human practices. They are historically defined as are all human practices. Therefore, the specific content of Christian virtues is determined always in relation to the historical understanding of the believing community. The notion of virtue itself requires a community that shares a common tradition. It also requires some shared vision of the purpose or meaning of human life which is informed by that tradition. Thus, virtues are never simply momentary or individual practices. They are practices which are affirmed by a particular community as authentic expressions of its tradition and its hope. Virtues then are the practices of a community by which that community bears witness to its memory and its vision.

What the Christian community has seen and heard in Jesus Christ is the unlimited love of God for humankind and the world. The one who creates the world in love creatively enters into the world, gives herself to be with the world, and receives the world to herself. Faith is confidence in God's loving intention and action in the world and God's acceptance of the world in loving forgiveness. It is confidence that God is everywhere acting creatively and redemptively for the world, and it is also belief that God calls us to work with her here and now.

None of this is meant to imply that faith is a naive belief that all is well and all will end well. Faith is only trust in God's promise in Jesus Christ that she is working with the world for good everywhere and always. Faith, then, is belief in genuine possibility for human beings in the world.

The virtue of faith is always accompanied by hope for the future of the world. Christian hope is hope that looks beyond any present toward the future of greater fulfillment in Jesus Christ. It is the ever present readiness to believe that the future may be a time when the goodness of God's creative-redemptive love is made known more comprehensively. As such, it is not hope based on what is now seen and heard in the world as such. It is hope in the midst of hopelessness. Christian hope is faith standing firm before futility. In other words, the hope of the Christian community is hope against hope.

Through its own inner life, the practice of the Christian community will be to share its faith and hope with the world. Called forth by its faith and hope, the Christian community is by nature evangelical. It is of the nature of faith and hope to engage in the mutual speech and hearing that will engender hope in all communities for our common future together.

But faith and hope are not merely matters of speech and hearing. These virtues are practiced by living as if the possibilities of the future are already present. The virtues of faith and hope are the practice of living as if a world which to all intents and purposes is alien, strange, and threatening is a place given us to live. It is living as if the poor are being liberated from their isolation and injustice. In these ways, faith and hope are "living the future" in the present, with all the risk which that entails. They are the practice of claiming the world for the possibilities of a common redemptive future.

Traditionally, living the future of redemptive possibility has been called the life of love. In our present situation, we believe that this life of love has at least three dimensions.

First, the life of love is life *in* God's love. The community that lives in God's love is therefore a grateful community whose primary corporate act is giving thanks to the one who has given such gifts to the community itself and to the world. The thanksgiving of the Christian community is a joyful anticipation of where it is going and the confidence in its perseverance to the end. But thanksgiving is not simply for good fortune nor is it for achievement. It is always only for God's goodness. As such, it will be a reminder that the people of God will be characterized by a certain humility about themselves and their accomplishments. Because they know that God's gift is free to everyone, they will also have a fundamental aversion to claims of superiority and exclusiveness. Moreover, thanksgiving is not simply for being with each other, it is also for being in and with the world. It is not for the human world alone but for the whole world, including the complex natural milieu, living and nonliving. The community stands in awe and views with grateful wonder the whole of this gift, recognizing that the possibility of human community is dependent upon the supporting and enriching whole of the one divinely created order.

Second, the life of love is living for justice for all the world's people. It is living with a global reach which recognizes no national boundaries to its concern for the victims of injustice. Christian love knows injustice to be the intolerable estrangement of one from the other. Injustice is the refusal to see the other one as the one with me, and to see myself as one for the other. Injustice is the name given to the denial of community, and that is a refusal of the gift of God to us. At its base, then, injustice is no mere moral problem, some defect that could be remedied easily by plans and programs alone. Injustice is the refusal of God's gift, a denial of our hope in God for one another. As such, it is the opposite of love and in no way belongs in the world. It is intolerable to the community of faith, for it is not only a failure to love but also an intrusion into our being, a rupture in the fellowship of the world with God. It represents, therefore, a loss of both faith and hope.

Third, the life of love is care for the whole earth. It is a life of tenderness toward God's creatures, a life of joy in the beauty of creation. It is a life of wonder at the scope of the gift and a life of careful stewardship of that gift. The life of love is living permanently in the world as receivers and not as owners of the earth, because there is no necessity to own something that will be given again and again. That enables the life of love to be the life of sharing ourselves and what we have fully with one another and with the world. As one trusts God to be faithful to her promise, one is freed from the necessity of struggling against others to secure one's own place and of protecting one's own life at the expense of all life. In other words, one is free to be fully oneself, created to be in full fellowship and partnership with God in God's creative and redemptive action for the world.

When life is understood this way, the world is also freed for the human community. It is not as though life is sacred. Only God is sacred, and the people of God understand that the life of nonhuman creatures is also for humanity. Love for the nonhuman world is not superstitious and sentimental. Nonhuman life in the world, to be sure, has a right to be here, and love for the world requires a sense of community with the other creatures of God. They are not here to be destroyed willy-nilly, but they do not exist finally for themselves alone. Like all of God's creatures, they are for life, and they exist for the fulfillment of the whole. Wanton destruction of the creatures, land, and forest is not merely unwise, as if the only problem for us were our own survival. Such care-less disregard of our nonhuman neighbors is a manifestation of our desire to impose our necessity on the world. It is an attempt to make the gift of God our own possession, to wrest from God what is God's and make it exclusively our own. That is a refusal to live in God's love and to trust God's promise.

The community of holiness is the community of faith, hope, and love. These virtues are central to our memory, and they form the context within which we conduct our lives in response to our present situation. The practice of these virtues is the announcement of our vision of the future. As such, these virtues are at once the living word of the church as the community of holiness and the marks of a Christian character.

11. *The Church as Worshiping Community*

We have offered ten images of the church that we believe are appropriate to direct its energies. But no one of them focuses on worship, the central act of the church, that activity apart from which the church cannot be a church at all. The community gathers to celebrate and real-ize God's work and to remind itself of how it has discovered that work in God's history with Israel, as illumined and focused in Jesus Christ. It does so by grace as one expression of the creative and redemptive work to which it points. Through this act it recognizes itself as a human com-munity; reaffirms its intention to be a caring and evangelistic commu-nity; acknowledges that its life must be for the whole world, with special attention to the poor, to oppressed races, and to women; and symbolizes and commits itself to the task of integration, continuing repentance, and the actualization of holiness.

Worship is directed toward God and not, in the first instance, to the forming of the church's self-understanding. Christians praise God be-cause God is worthy of praise; give thanks because God has given so much; confess their sins because in God's presence these are known as a breach of community with her; and receive forgiveness because it is God's nature to forgive. But because the God who is worshiped is the God of Abraham, Isaac, Jacob, and Jesus, the Christian worship can never separate the relation to God from the relation to neighbors. The God who is worshiped is also the life of all things that live and the light that enlightens everyone. Christians cannot love God except as they also love their neighbor. The sin that violates their community with God is the failure to meet the needs of their fellow creatures. Worship directed to God in such a way as to turn attention away from the world that God creates and redeems is not Christian worship. Christian worship never separates the celebration of God's work now transpiring in the congrega-tion from the remembrance of how God has worked in the history that has formed it. It is this history that now guides the church to the discernment of God's present gift and call.

Although worship is directed to God and not to forming and refining the church's self-understanding—indeed, precisely for this reason it determines how Christians think of God and hence of themselves, individually and corporately. Worship is the practice of the community of the people of God by which they reaffirm their tradition as a living tradition, one in which God is met ever anew. It is thus the context within which the character of the Christian life is formed. Because Christian worship is corporate, it bonds together the worshipers. At worship there are nurtured in the community shared beliefs from which should emerge new impetus for Christian practice in the world; and the engendering of Christian practice in the world is what is known as mission. The church as a worshiping community is always a church in mission.

Because worship is so fundamental to the church and so powerful a force in molding it, the church's health depends on the appropriateness of what is said and done during its services of corporate worship. If what is celebrated is not the creative and redemptive work of God but rather the achievements of the community, the worship is not Christian. If what is celebrated is only what God does in and through the community, and not the creative and redemptive work of God in the whole world, the worship is not Christian. If worship makes the congregation content to minister only to its own needs, the worship is not Christian. If worship segregates itself from the real world and produces an artificial and separate community, it is not Christian. We place the image of the church as a worshiping community last not only to highlight its decisive importance, but also to make clear that the worship that is the heart of the church's life must be *Christian* worship, worship informed by the other images of what the church is to be.

For example, if Christians are to understand themselves as globally connected, then worship must broaden their horizons to a fully global context. It will do so to whatever extent it moves them to accept God's truth as judgment on their own present conceptions of truth and to bring their own conceptions into conformity with God's truth. If we are to act for a unified world, our worship must direct us to God as the creator and redeemer of an interdependent creation, who values all living things. If we are to act for the poor, we must worship the God who has revealed herself as for and with the poor. If we are to be an inclusive community, we must worship the God who has called one church into being and suffers in its fragmentation along with the sinful suffering of the divided churches.

In baptism we are reminded of our need for forgiveness, and we are given firm assurance of that forgiveness by the symbolic enactment of cleansing. We enact our bond with the history of the faithful community and, particularly in infant baptism, we enact our responsibility to one another and for one another, while at the same time we recall our dependence on the grace of God and the faithfulness of other people of God.

In the eucharist, we present again the supreme act of God's love and the obedience of Jesus Christ that have freed us from bondage to our past and have opened to us new possibilities for the future. Participants are reminded that there is pain and suffering around them, and they are invited to share in that pain and suffering, in the world and for the world. They are revisited by grace as both a gift and a call.

Protestantism has generally emphasized the central role of preaching in worship. Because preaching takes place in the context of worship, it shares in the general orientation toward God. But its special role in worship is to address the worshiper with the word of God. Its distinctive function is to make explicit what it means to live from some portion of the shared memory in relation to some aspect of contemporary experience. At its best, it not only repeats what the worshipers know, but it also expands their horizons of understanding and stimulates reflection and decision. Preaching can call for a decision more specific than the re-identification with the community. Although the other features of worship make real what is remembered, preaching juxtaposes what Christians have learned through their memory with what they learn from other sources and in daily life. The task of preaching is to enable the hearers, as they stand before God, to incorporate into their Christian memories those truths that come to them from other sources, some of which appear antithetical to their Christian memories. In this way, preaching helps expand the hearers' memories. They learn at this time to repent for those aspects of their remembered history in which they once took pride or to introduce into their inner histories elements of the past that heretofore had appeared alien.

Preaching does this best when it expands the hearers' freedom to reflect. It does this by offering new ways of thinking about troubling questions or pointing them to previously unfamiliar ideas. In this way, their freedom is expanded as they are presented with opportunities for growth. If the reality renewed through worship is not to become totally isolated from the reality pressed on all of us by the contemporary world, it must be expanded to include the truth that the contemporary world has learned and taught. As this happens in the congregation's shared experience, the remainder of worship can express this enlarged and transformed memory.

The church's identity is its shared memory of the history of God's work with Israel as it appears to Christians through Jesus Christ. That memory directs the church to discern God's present workings in itself and in the whole world. When the church is healthy, it responds openly to God's present call and allows itself to be created and redeemed anew. It is thus in worship that this identity is renewed, reshaped, deepened, and transformed.

Chapter IV

Professional Church Leadership

We have described what we mean by the church's being the community whose history has been determined by the memory of Jesus Christ. It is that people who have committed themselves to keeping alive his memory by corporately representing that memory in worship, teaching, and service to the world. We have also analyzed the present world-historical context of the church and identified some of the global issues that dominate our understanding of our world situation. Finally, by looking at the world situation from a perspective formed by the church's internal history, we have tried to imagine the future of the church in this world. We have proposed certain images of the church that function normatively for the living practice of the community formed in the memory of Israel's life with God centering in Jesus Christ. In other words, we have projected into the future our theology of the ministry of the church in the world.

We now turn to the question of leadership for the church. Given the general identity of the Christian community and the implications of that identity, what sort of leadership does it need?

The question of leadership is a very broad one. Although we shall focus on the tasks of professional leadership, it should be understood that in our view, leadership for the churches is by no means simply professional leadership. The church's leadership has been, and ought to be, also the responsibility of those persons whose particular vocation is not professional church leadership. Countless persons in the congregations regularly give instruction in the faith, provide counsel and guidance to one another, and contribute significantly to the worship of the church. Most of them would not be considered professional leaders of the church by any definition, but without their contributions the church would not continue to live out its faithful witness. It is, in fact, the nonprofessional leadership of the churches which makes professional leadership possible. Still, the churches have always appointed leaders to perform certain representative functions. This has been true since New Testament times, and it would be naive to believe that the churches can operate today without strong and competent professionals. In our highly differentiated social structures, human institutions require specially prepared leaders. The church as a fully human institution requires them no less than any other.

By professional leadership, we do *not* mean only ordained clergy. Though what we shall say about leadership style and substance clearly applies to ordained persons, it applies to lay professional leaders as well. Differences in the understanding of ordination among the denominations complicate this picture, but the issues involved do not bear directly on the topics of this chapter.

1. The Emerging New Professional

We addressed the problem of professional leadership in Chapter I. There we examined various characterizations of professional church leaders which have emerged in changing historical contexts in the United States. We have argued that certain of these characterizations became dominant for periods of time and then faded from view as the socio-political landscape altered and the perceptions of the role and authority of religion in the United States underwent significant modifications.

The result, as we noted, was to create confusion in the churches and in the society at large about what was the professional leadership of the church today, and especially of the pastoral ministry. Without any consensus in the churches, the inevitable has happened. The expectations for leadership in the society as a whole have increasingly been adopted as normative for church leadership as well. Following the general pattern of bureaucratization, the churches, too, have focused on routinized problem solving in the organization and maintenance of their institutions as the chief locus of leadership effectiveness. In other words, the minister as Manager is the strongest candidate for the dominant image of professional leadership.

We have already indicated our dissatisfaction with this state of affairs. Although it is true that professional church leaders must be good at organizational development and maintenance, the modern idea of the professional manager, as one who solves problems by the application of scientific theory, is simply not adequate as an image for church leadership.

There are strong indications that the dominant understanding of management is perceived to be inadequate outside the church as well. Even in business, in which the modern idea of the professional has exerted its greatest influence, there is widespread restlessness with the prevailing view that the effective manager is mainly an expert in conceptual problem solving for a specified pool of clients.

Harold Leavitt, in his Stockton Lecture for 1983, sounds this note of dissatisfaction with great clarity.[1] He notes a growing perception that management requires much more than skill at conceptualizing problems

---

[1] Harold J. Leavitt, "Management and Management Education," The Stockton Lecture, London Business School, March 16, 1983. Cf. also Robert Reich, *The Next American Frontier* (New York: Penguin Books, 1984), esp. Chaps. 4–7. Our colleague, Peter

and solutions to problems. He argues that the failure of American management to develop a broader understanding of its tasks has led to a worldwide decline in performance and prestige. What is required is a recasting of the understanding of the Manager by giving attention to management tasks which have, to this point, been largely ignored by management educators.

Leavitt proposes a three-part model of management. It consists of *problem-solving, implementing,* and *pathfinding.* The emphasis on the parts can be charted historically. From about 1910 to 1960, there was very little emphasis on either implementation or pathfinding. The expert problem-solver reigned supreme.

> From time study to the assembly line to industrial engineering to more recent forms of systems analysis, the trend was toward planning and systemizing, with ever increasingly specialized staff groups to collect the data and do the analysis that would in effect dictate the "proper" decision.[2]

In the early 1950s a few critical voices began to suggest that management was not all problem solving. They contended that management required implementation skills, the ability to get things done. Managers had to enter into the messy world of human motivation, persuasion, and negotiation. A purely formal solution to a particular problem is of little use unless there is a corresponding ability to generate the human processes of interaction which flow from the drawing board to the product. Managers as implementers are those who must get other people involved in action based on their best thinking about a particular problem or problem set.

We shall have something to say in Section 3 about the minister as an implementer. At this point, we simply note Leavitt's comment that the criticism of the lack of implementation skills so prevalent in the 1950s was soon drowned by a new tide of emphasis on problem-solving. Again rationalization and routinization became prominent features of thinking about managerial problems. This time it was the technology of decision making which dominated managerial education. Human emotion was simply "noise" in the system. So management education became the scene of conflict between the implementers and the problem solvers, but in the end the problem solvers won the day. This is most clearly seen in the curricula of top-rated American business schools. Leavitt estimates that about 80 percent of the courses in these schools are currently concerned with analytical problem-solving. The newest move has been one toward greater emphasis on quantification and operational programming.[3]

Drucker, has sounded a similar theme since 1954. Cf. Peter Drucker, *The Practice of Management* (New York: Harper & Row, 1954) esp. pp. 341ff.

[2] Leavitt, op. cit.

[3] Ibid.

In the midst of all this movement toward a refined science of decision-making or managerial problem-solving, there does remain some interest in *implementation*. But what is completely missing is any emphasis on *pathfinding*. Leavitt believes this to be the chief weakness of American management education, and consequently of American management itself. Leavitt argues that the manager as pathfinder is absolutely essential for the success of institutions. Pathfinders are persons with a vision of what the institution is to become, of where it ought to be in the future. They are persons with passionate commitments, able to inspire others to share their commitments. It is the pathfinders who keep raising the question of institutional purpose even in the midst of their work of problem-solving and implementation.

Leavitt concludes that good management must include attention to all three aspects of the managerial task. Managers must be problem-solvers—clear, rational, orderly thinkers about organizational problems; they must be implementers, able to engage others persuasively and creatively to get things done; and they must be the pathfinders, those who call forth allegiance to a vision of what can be and ought to be, the purpose of the organization.

In many respects, the needs of the churches for leadership parallel Leavitt's suggestions for effective business management. The church as a human institution requires leaders who are skilled in management. They must be able to identify problems and propose solutions. The congregation must be involved in implementing the solutions. But above all else, the leadership of the church requires vision. Church members expect their leaders to be something more than problem-solvers and implementers. They expect them to be able to give guidance to their own reflection about who Christians are and what this Christian identity implies for their living practice in the world. Even more, the members of the churches expect their leaders to be deeply affected by and formed in the memory of Jesus Christ so that they, to some degree, embody their vision for the church and act out their own commitment to its ministry with comprehensive integrity. In a word, church members expect their leaders not only to be skilled practitioners but leaders with a Christian vision. In Leavitt's terms, the greatest need of the churches is for pathfinders.

This does not mean, of course, that the church leader's only task is to conceptualize the future of the church. Every leader has specific and immediate responsibilities. In the case of pastors, their daily work involves them as counselors, administrators, pastoral visitors and worship leaders, along with a variety of other important functions. They are problem-solvers and implementers. To some degree, they must be responsible for decisive leadership in all of these functions of congregational life. Yet this is not what is determinative and primary for Christian ministry, in any of its forms. What is distinctive is that all of these functions are determined by the conceptions that the minister shares with the congregation concerning Christian identity and practice. In light of this, counseling is not just counseling; it is a function of a caring community formed in the memory of Jesus Christ. And church management is not simply institutional management; it is the attempt to deploy the churches' resources with a view to authentic Christian practice by a transformed and transforming community.

What we shall propose, therefore, are two images of those who minister as professional church leaders that will capture the reality of the church as we have described it. The first of these images is the minister as *Practical Christian Thinker*. It is here that we shall attend to the pathfinding aspect of ministerial leadership. The second image is the minister as *Reflective Practitioner*. Following the lead of Donald Schoen, we shall attend here to the question of a leadership style that is suitable for an institution that needs to find and implement solutions to practical problems as efficiently as possible. After discussing these two images separately, we shall combine them into one, broader understanding of the ministry—the minister as *Practical Theologian*.

2. The Practical Christian Thinker

Like all institutions, the church needs pathfinders. But the pathfinding necessary to the church is distinctive. First, as we have urged in Chapter III, the envisionment of goals for the church, however local and concrete, requires sensitivity to the global context. It requires also that this context be viewed in an appropriately Christian way. The professional leader should be able to help the congregation determine what a Christian perspective on this global situation should be. For example, the situation is viewed by some in the United States as a struggle of the free world against a demonic totalitarian Communism. By others it is perceived as a struggle for freedom from hunger and oppression on the part of the mass of the people against an alliance of superpowers with local exploiters. Which of these, or other, interpretations is more appropriate for the Christian is a matter of great importance influencing definitions of problems at all levels. The Christian leader should help other Christians perceive the situation as Christians.

Such a formulation of the leader's task seems to imply that there is one Christian perception of each situation. If to say this meant that all equally Christian persons see the world in the same way, this would clearly be false. One cannot, therefore, provide only one description of *the* Christian perception of our world. What Christians have distinctively in common is not shared ideas, theories, and principles, but a shared internal history, or at least a shared center of internal history. Even that history is read and appropriated by Christians in diverse ways.

How to read it, how to appropriate it, are questions that are continually in dispute. But the history is not for that reason without its own power to form those who acknowledge it.

The internal history of a community is like a personal life story. It has effectiveness in shaping responses to new situations even when it is not remembered. But it functions more healthfully when it is restored to memory. How it is recalled, remembered, and recounted also deeply affects the way the present situation is viewed. Assuming that for all Christians, insofar as they are Christian, the story determines their identity, the struggle within the church is always over how it is to be read and understood.

In this regard, the importance of corporate worship, and especially of preaching, can hardly be exaggerated. How the congregation appropriates its inner history depends largely on how it is expressed in the worship it shares and the preaching it hears over the years. This is where its common identity originates. If that preaching substitutes the prejudices of the preacher for serious wrestling with the meaning of the community's history, especially its origins in Israel as appropriated through Jesus Christ, the congregation's identity will become vapid. Its distinctiveness in relation to other voluntary associations will become tenuous. It may try to substitute a common purpose, common values, or common beliefs for a common internal history, but the prospects for success in such an undertaking are poor. Either it will simply express the ideas of the age, or it will be driven to sectarian rigidities. The healthy pluralism of a community formed by a common history cannot be recovered on other grounds. Christian vitality will be lost by either evaporation or rigidification.

For the church to be healthy, its leadership must constantly renew, deepen, and expand its corporate memory and help all the members to view the contemporary situation accurately as that memory illumines it. Although an external historian can contribute much to this process, it is finally only the believer, the one whose own life and thought are formed by this memory, who can lead. How the situation appears to the believer can be discovered only by the believer who looks at the situation. It cannot be deduced from doctrines or principles. But how it looks to the believer will depend on the way the internal history of the community is understood. Believers can help one another to understand that history better and hence to perceive the situation more appropriately.

The most important single way in which memory of the past illumines the present is through the relevance of past occurrences to contemporary events. The memory of the lowly birth of Jesus, his baptism by John, his temptations in the wilderness, his controversies, his healing of the sick, his passion for the poor, his setting his face to go to Jerusalem, his cleansing the temple, his last supper, his struggle in Gethsemane, his betrayal and crucifixion, or his resurrection may provide the needed illumination and guidance for the present. Or it may be one of the great historical events in the life of Israel—Abraham's journey, Joseph's forgiveness of his brothers, the time of slavery in Egypt, the story of Moses and the Exodus, the conquest of the promised land, the rise and fall of the two kingdoms, the great prophets, exile, and return. Or stories from Christian history may seem to be the best ones, beginning with the Acts of the Apostles.

The very power of this most concrete form of the story from which we live suggests that it must be used with care. The history of the church is replete with instances in which harm has been done by unwise selection and the resulting distortion of perceptions. There are several checks. First, for Christians, any story must be read in relation to Jesus Christ. That center to internal history forbids any self-aggrandizing use of any part of that history. Second, the scholarly study of our history brings us to a more accurate recounting. We are helped to distinguish fact from fiction, not in order to depreciate the fictional stories that are so important in our heritage, but to read them as fiction and to let them affect us as such. Third, the further scholarly task of the study of the history of the ways these stories have been interpreted and used both widens our horizons and prevents us from committing errors that have long since been detected and exposed. Because it is unrealistic to expect most Christians to go far into the scholarly literature, the church needs professional leaders who can help form its memory in light of this extensive research.

The internal history that gives identity to the church is not limited to stories of this sort. From very early days Christians strove to understand the whole of things in light of their history. The writing of systematic theologies expresses this passion for comprehensiveness and coherence of vision. These theologies and their profound effects on the church are just as much a part of our internal history as are events of the sort mentioned above. The drive to understand conceptually and clearly pervades much of that internal history and shapes many Christians today as well. Past and present efforts to conceptualize the meaning of living and thinking as Christians are also capable of illuminating the situation in which Christians now find themselves and indicating the goals they should pursue. To seek to understand our present reality in light of the history of theology is not to try to apply theory, but it requires at least as full an understanding of theology as would be the case if theology functioned as a theory base for practice.

Our internal history molds our perceptions and goals in other ways as well. Perhaps the most important of these governed our work in Chapter III. Out of our reading of Christian history and the discernment of the present situation to which that has led us, we proposed guiding images of the church. These are justified only as they commend themselves to others who are informed by Christian history and allow it to shape their perception in the present. When a community can agree upon such guiding images, its ability to act cohesively is greatly increased. For interpreting such guiding images as well, the church needs professional leadership.

Partly because of the dominance of the modern model of the professional as the applier of theory, and the inability of ministers to shape their practice accordingly, the church's ability to act with integrity, that is, in terms of its Christian identity, has eroded radically in recent generations. Indeed, no problem is more urgent for the church than to recover its ability to direct its practice consciously in a Christian way. Its main need now is to renew identity and to act according to that identity, and for such renewal and action, leaders are required.

The most important requirements of the professional Christian leader, then, are: first, a clear Christian identity; second, an extensive and reflective understanding of what constitutes that identity; third, self-consciousness as to how that Christian identity shapes perception of the present concrete world-historical situation; fourth, wise discernment of the implications of this Christian perception for action.

The principal focus here is on thinking, but the thinking in question is oriented to practice. Hence, we suggest that the minister should be a practical thinker. But everything depends on the identity about which, and in terms of which, the minister thinks. If the church is to be the church, that identity must be Christian. Hence we propose that the professional leaders of the church should be Practical Christian Thinkers.

3. The Reflective Practitioner

Though we have insisted that practical Christian thinking is the church's greatest need and, therefore, the first task of the minister, we do not intend by this to suggest that thinking should be done independently of the minister's functions in the life of the congregation. Indeed, practical Christian thinking is thinking about such practice as well. By practice we mean every Christian's practice of Christian vocation. The vocation of church leaders is the same as that of all Christians, namely, to live as Christians in their vocational settings. The only difference is that church professionals exercise their special calling chiefly within the church. Hence, understanding the church is especially important to the right exercise of their leadership. Also, the church's leaders must be skilled in helping others in the church develop their Christian identity and understandng so that together they may act in a Christian way.

The church is a human community of mutual caring. As such, it shares some needs with other human institutions that are not Christian.

As we have already indicated, the need for pathfinding is shared by all human institutions. In other words, what we have described as practical thinking is essential if institutions are to remain vital.

But more than thinking about practice is required. Leaders may project fine visions of the future and lofty claims of purpose. They may be capable of formulating plans to get from here to there, but unless their style of leadership motivates, inspires, and involves other human beings in carrying out those plans, they will remain visionaries—not leaders. As Leavitt argues, no problem-solver or pathfinder who is not also an implementer can give leadership. In fact, implementation, problem-solving and pathfinding are only analytically discrete. In practice, these tasks overlap. Thus, the leader with a vision is always asking the question of means and the sensitive leader is always reassessing the situation to make sure that the means are not only appropriate to the end but also effective for concrete problem-solving.[4] In other words, not only do effective manager/leaders engage in practical thinking. They are ever involved in what Donald Schoen has called *reflective practice*.[5] At every step of the way, the leader is thinking about the nature of certain problems of practice, the means of resolving those problems, and the way in which this mode of practice serves the vision of the institution. Thus Practical Christian Thinkers reflect not only *about* practice. They also reflect *in* practice. And this comprehensive practical reflection is characterized by a particular style, one which is appropriate to the character of leadership required by a human community of mutual caring.

Though the mode of reflective practice applies across the board to the functions of ministry, the managerial and counseling functions will serve to illustrate what we mean.

As we have said earlier, by the middle of the 1950s the minister as Manager and Counselor had become dominant in the self-understanding of many practitioners. Since professional leaders were aware that church members had the same need for counseling as others did, and perceived that church institutions required managerial skills similar to those needed in other institutions, it is not surprising that the modern professional paradigm dominated their self-understanding and shaped the expectations of congregations as well. Thus there arose a fascination with the "techniques" of management and counseling that led many ministers to accept rather uncritically models based on that paradigm. This meant that ministers were seen more and more as experts who knew a theory (technique) that they could apply to a problem identified by their pool of clients (individual members in distress or church organizations in disarray). As inadequate as it was, the model held the promise of

---

[4] Ibid.
[5] Schoen, op. cit.

recovering some semblance of authority grounded in technical expertise to replace the authority that the religious leadership had lost under the impact of secularism. But as we have seen, it was an illusory gain. As Schoen has pointed out, and as increasing numbers of practitioners find, the modern paradigm of the professional is highly problematic. It simply does not fit their experience in practice. This is true even in those professions in which there is considerable use in practice of research-based theory. It is especially true in a profession such as ministry where the nature of research-based theory is not clear and what is designated as theory is only tangentially related to practice. Of the so-called hard professions, Schoen has written:

> In some parts of some practices—medicine, agronomy, engineering, dentistry, management, for example—practitioners can and do make use of knowledge generated by university-based researchers. But even in these professions, large zones of practice present problematic situations which do not lend themselves to applied science. What is more, there is a disturbing tendency for research and practice to follow divergent paths. Practitioners and researchers tend increasingly to live in different worlds, pursue different enterprises, and have little to say to one another. Teachers have gained relatively little from cognitive psychology; political and administrative practice has gained little from the policy sciences; and management science has contributed relatively little to the practice of management. The divergence of research and practice exacerbates the practitioner's dilemma which I have called "rigor or relevance," and tempts the practitioner to force practice situations into molds derived from research.[6]

It is important to understand the reasons for the failure of the modern paradigm of the professional. The application of theory to practice works well when the problems presented for solution are unambiguous and the theory that is scientifically established is directly applicable. But the real world is not composed of discrete sets of self-defining problems. Problematic situations are multifaceted, and the clarification of the interconnected problems themselves is an activity that cannot be understood as an application of theory. Those professionals who insist on the received model are likely to be too much influenced in their formulation of problems by the theories with which they are familiar, obscuring complexities that do not fit. Even in medicine, in which the application of theory has been effective, there is now a widespread recognition that treating a patient as a case pertinent to a particular theory is often destructive. Attempting to model other professions on this paradigm has been a mistake.

The second reason that the applied theory approach is defective is that it directs attention away from how skills are actually learned and

6 Ibid., p. 308.

developed. The best judgments of professionals are often based on types of knowledge gained through experience that are not consciously entertained. The articulation of this knowledge, if it occurs at all, often takes place after the fact. Therefore idealizing the application of consciously entertained theory throws little light on the way the best professionals operate. Again, this is true even for physicians, who often size up the whole situation of the patient and treat him or her accordingly by insights that have never been theoretically formulated. It is more predominantly true in most other professions.

Schoen proposes that professionals will understand themselves and function better if they recognize themselves, not as appliers of theory but as "reflective practitioners." This model in no way depreciates thought, but the understanding of thought is changed. Schoen writes:

> When we reject the traditional view of professional knowledge, recognizing that practitioners may *become* reflective researchers in situations of uncertainty, instability, uniqueness, and conflict, we have recast the relationship between research and practice. For on this perspective, research is an activity of practitioners. It is triggered by features of the practice situation, undertaken on the spot, and immediately linked to action. There is no question of an "exchange" between research and practice or of "implementation" of research results, when the frame- or theory-testing experiments of the practitioner at the same time transform the practice situation. Here the exchange between research and practice is immediate, and reflection-in-action is its own implementation.[7]

The implications of the model of the professional as Reflective Practitioner might appear on the surface to question the desirability of having any professional schools at all. But Schoen believes that in addition to the reflection-in-action characteristic of the work of the professional as reflective practitioner, there is also "reflective research" that is properly carried on in other contexts, such as formal educational settings.[8]

We shall attend to the role of reflective research in Chapter V, as we discuss the components of the seminary curriculum. It will become clear, however, that reflective research is not related to practice as "theory." This is one point at which the model of the reflective practitioner departs sharply from the modern professional paradigm.

The modern professionals see themselves as experts possessing a theoretical knowledge that their clients or patients do not have. They ask the clients or patients to trust their expertise and surrender themselves into their professional hands. They thus diminish the ability of those they serve to understand their world or even to care for themselves. Reflective practitioners, on the other hand, work with those they serve. They offer

[7] Ibid., pp. 308–9.
[8] Ibid., p. 309.

insights and knowledge gained mainly through experience in similar situations. They share this and come to decisions in collaboration with those who seek their help. Thus the result is an enhancement of the ability of those they serve to understand their world and care for themselves.[9]

It is our contention that the ministry has never been, should not be, and cannot be, professional in the strict sense of the modern paradigm. Ministers do *not* simply apply theory in order to solve problems. In some contexts elements of such application can, of course, be helpful. But ministers who consider what they are doing as applying theory will damage their ministry. On the other hand, ministry has been practice that has been more or less reflective, and it can be improved by being more reflective in certain ways. We propose that ministers adopt for themselves the paradigm Schoen now recommends for all professionals, that of the Reflective Practitioner.

Given the hegemony of the applied theory model, ministers have felt that they should be applying their theology to their practice. But they have not been able to do so. The relation of Christian doctrine to church practice can only occasionally be one of applying theory. There is a remarkable essay by Karl Barth in which he argues from the resurrection of Jesus Christ to the necessity for the Anglo-Saxon powers to go to war against Hitler. But few would regard this as a model for decision-making in the churches.

The discipline of Christian ethics has sometimes been understood as the bridge between theology and practice. But in fact this discipline has not been able to achieve this goal. In general it has understood appropriate Christian practice as application of theory, in this case ethical theory. Recognizing that church doctrine cannot provide the needed basis, it has developed its own principles and its own theory of application. But it has found it difficult to decide whether there are any distinctively Christian ethical principles or theories of their application. It often seems that Christian ethicists simply call on the church to be ethical according to the standards of the general or philosophical community. Furthermore, the effort to apply principles to specific situations founders in that the discipline of ethics comes to bear only when the problematic of the situation is clear and clearly fits the established theory, whereas in this chaotic world, such situations are the rare exceptions.

Again, recognition of the limitations of the model of applied theory may help to overcome this problem. Christian theology, whether official credal formulations or the speculation of contemporary influential Christian thinkers, cannot be readily applied to the complex, concrete situations in which people live and make decisions. Ethical principles,

9 Ibid., p. 300.

whether distinctively Christian or not, face similar difficulties. Neither theology nor ethics is irrelevant. But skill in making Christian decisions is not the same as the knowledge of how to apply Christian theory to already defined problems.

In recent times pastors seeking to be responsibly professional, and recognizing that there is no Christian theory for them to apply, have turned to the psychological and sociological disciplines for the theory they need. They have learned much that has been useful in filling certain roles. But the overall results have not been impressive. Ministers have sought to counsel members of the congregation according to patterns that are used by secular counselors, and they have tried to learn from management theory, developed with business in mind, how to manage churches. Schoen points out that the study of psychological and sociological theory has had minimum benefit in these secular professions. Its effect on ministers is highly ambiguous. As ministers come to understand themselves as reflective practitioners, perhaps many of the distortions introduced into the profession by the theory-practice model can be overcome.

The image of the Reflective Practitioner is extremely helpful, then, for understanding how the problems of institutional management and interpersonal dynamics are most effectively defined and how solutions to such problems may be more adequately designed and implemented. The church leader as a Reflective Practitioner can become a cooperating and supporting leader in a group process that includes the "clients" at every point as conversation partners. The model also emphasizes flexibility in problem definition and situational analysis as well as proposed responses. As Schoen puts it, the Reflective Practitioner remains in "conversation" with the client and the situation, and the outcome of reflective practice thus always contains in it a dimension different from that which might be anticipated by a more rigid application of theory to practice. In a word, reflective action is always open to surprise.[10] As such, it is not only an exercise in problem solving and implementation for and with clients, but it is also an ongoing process of self-education by the practitioners themselves.[11]

What Schoen calls reflective practice is one form of what is often spoken of as *praxis*. That term has a rich history and can be used quite appropriately. In some of its uses it is broader than reflective practice and tends to be sufficiently inclusive as to contain practical thinking as well. But on the whole the discussion of praxis has neglected the question

---

[10] Ibid., pp. 295, 296, 328.
[11] Ibid., p. 299. Cf. also Edward Farley, "Theology and Practice Outside the Clerical Paradigm," in Don Browning, ed., *Practical Theology* (San Francisco: Harper & Row, 1983).

of normative identity and the distinction between practical thinking and reflective practice that we have made here. We believe that this distinction can be brought more adequately to the fore by using, at least for a while, new terminology.

4. *The Practical Theologian*

We have proposed thus far two images for professional ministers: the Practical Christian Thinker and the Reflective Practitioner. In the first, we have focused on the distinctive base' for the practice of *Christian* leadership. In the second, our attention was upon the reflective style appropriate to professional leadership of the church. Thus, though the Practical Christian Thinker and the Reflective Practitioner are intimately related to practice, they are still distinct and cannot simply be collapsed together.

One cannot subsume the Practical Christian Thinker under the Reflective Practitioner. To do so would be to lose the distinctiveness of the Christian practice of church leadership. It is extremely important that professional activities not be allowed to become autonomous from practical Christian thinking. This is the thinking relevant for establishing the mission of the church and its priorities as well as bringing the Christian perspective to bear on major issues facing the world. Pastoral care and church management must be informed by the church's special sensitivities, goals, and priorities. Moreover, practical Christian thinking may determine the guidelines for Christian practice, including action the church takes on behalf of the world.

It would also be a mistake to try to subsume reflective practice under practical Christian thinking. This could lead to the false assumption that thinking *about* practice is all that is required, whereas we have insisted that thinking *in* practice or reflecting *while* practicing is equally important. The Practical Christian Thinker could thus fall victim again to the old professional paradigm. Those who know more than others do about any matter are always tempted to assume that they know all there is to know. Moreover, those who have reflected systematically *on* Christian practice are often apt to see themselves as somehow the theoreticians and to make others responsible for "applying" their theory. As we have seen in the case of business management, the old professional paradigm waits in the wings to reassert itself. This hardly needs to be said to a community that is now under assault from the old paradigm in its latest guise—the church growth movement. Again, the experts have the solution to certain clear specified managerial problems. If the "clients" will follow their instructions, the "problem" will be solved.

Some tension remains between reflective practice and practical Christian thinking. On the one hand, practical Christian thinking calls for bold vision, aggressive leadership, and strong commitment to genuine Christian practice. On the other hand, reflective practice calls for involvement of the whole community in practical thinking, and this means that leaders must also be collaborative and enabling as well. Yet these tensions will finally prove to be creative. The leadership of the Practical Christian Thinker must be consonant with the church's self-understanding as a human community. The Reflective Practitioner's practice must be grounded in the identity of the church and reflection on the implementation of that identity for life in the world.

Since these images are intimately connected and neither is adequate without the other, we propose a characterization of the minister for today which is capable of embracing both—the minister as *Practical Theologian*. Like all terms with a history, this one is problematic. The problems are of two sorts. First, "practical theology" has often been used interchangeably with "pastoral theology," and this has often focused on pastoral care. Pastoral care is certainly important, but it does not exhaust or even focus the whole of professional leadership in the church. If calling the professional minister a practical theologian strengthened the tendencies toward introversion of the church on the care of its own membership[12] we would be very distressed indeed.

However, there are significant movements today toward an inclusive use of "practical theology." When, for example, Johann Metz calls for practical theology to be accepted as foundational theology, his argument is not that pastoral theology should become the basic type of theology. Practical theology is critical reflection on the church's practice in view of the dangerous memory of the passion of Jesus. Church practice is evaluated in light of its role in the public world.[13]

Second, the image of the professional leader of the church as Practical Theologian seems to imply that practical theology is not relevant to other church leaders, whereas we do not wish to draw a sharp line. The same problem applied, in fact, to such other images as Master and Builder. Not all of the teachers of the church were professionals, and certainly volunteers contributed enormously to the tasks of building. Hence, we believe that we can propose the image of Practical Theologian for professional church leaders without implying that practical theology should be their exclusive prerogative.

At the same time, we do think that our definition of practical theology

---

[12] Cf. Thomas Oden, *Pastoral Theology: Essentials of Ministry* (San Francisco: Harper & Row, 1982).

[13] Johann Metz, *Faith in History and Society* (New York: Seabury Press, 1980), esp. pp. 88ff. See also Edward Farley, "Theology and Practice Outside the Clerical Paradigm," and Thomas Ogletree, "Dimensions of Practical Theology: Meaning, Action, Self," in Don Browning, ed., *Practical Theology* (San Francisco: Harper & Row, 1983), pp. 21ff. and 83ff.

indicates that it is especially needed by professional leaders. The practical Christian thinking which it signifies is important for all Christians and the distinctiveness of professionals is only that they have special responsibility to help others in this thinking. But reflective practice is a particular responsibility of the professional. Many church members will be called on to engage in reflective practice in their own professions, but the extent to which they should be expected to be involved in reflective practice with respect to their roles in the church must be limited. Since we have, somewhat arbitrarily, of course, defined the Practical Theologian as one whose reflective practice is primarily in the church, it does distinguish the professional church leader from most other equally faithful Christians.

There is an important respect in which this image of the professional minister as Practical Theologian differs from most of those treated by Osborn and summarized in Chapter I. Most of those focus on function. At different times and places, different functions have become dominant: Missionary, Revivalist, Pulpiteer, or Builder. Those functions were generally distinctive to the church and provided satisfactory Christian identities. They were called forth by the church's specific task in fulfillment of a clearly Christian mission. Osborn notes that in the twentieth century, caring for personal needs and institutional management have risen to dominance. Unlike their ancestors, these are only incidentally related to the church's mission. Rather, they correspond more to the needs of bourgeois individuals and voluntary associations generally. We do not dispute the importance of these functions, but we believe that identifying the professional ministry essentially in these terms is faithless to the proper understanding of the church.

One might try to restore a distinctively Christian identity to ministry by highlighting different roles. For example, one might suggest that the minister should be a spiritual director or a social activist, or some combination of these. That would indeed call for a ministry that is more distinctive and has clearer roots in Christian identity. But it would not solve the problem. Whatever label was used, ministers must still be both counselors and managers as well. To raise expectations about the primacy of other functions would simply lead to frustration. In any case, spiritual direction could become an expression of bourgeois culture, just as easily as counseling could. And the minister's correct relation to public affairs would need to be assessed before action for social justice could be proposed as the focus of ministerial activities.

We have responded to the problem in quite a different way. Practical theology is not one function along with others. It is a mode of reflection that continuously reevaluates the use of time and energy in and by the church in light of what the church truly is. A shift of roles or functions would not affect its appropriateness.

That does not mean that this is the proper understanding of the church's leadership in all times and places. The focus on practical theology expresses our judgment as to the greatest current danger of the church in North America. This danger is that it conforms to expectations established for it by a bourgeois society that stems from the Enlightenment and that it thereby will lose its Christian identity. This seems to be happening, and the church seems poorly equipped to clarify its Christian identity and to bring this to bear on its problems. To remedy this the church does not need to stress one function or another. Its need is to clarify its identity and to relate all of its functions to this identity as well as to determine their priorities. Perhaps in time, out of this clarification, a new image of professional leadership stressing one of those functions or another will emerge. What the church needs now is leadership in recovering its internal history so that its identity in the world as the church is strengthened and clarified.

We believe, in any case, that it is dangerous to identify professional ministry in terms of roles. There is no doubt that counseling a parishioner about marital problems is different from managing the church and that both differ from administering the sacraments. In this sense the minister certainly has many roles, but there is no one exhaustive enumeration of them. The effort to determine roles or functions is associated with the modern understanding of professionals as applying theory. This requires clear definitions of problems, and to attain this, professionals—in this case, ministers—must be clear as to what roles they are playing. But this cataloging fragments the minister's activity and raises questions as to whether there is any unifying ministerial identity. It is far better that the minister engage in diverse activities without trying to segregate them from one another. Pastoral care should not be absent when the minister presides at a planning session, and concern for the right understanding of the gospel or the proper ordering of the church should play its role in pastoral counseling. No opportunity for teaching or spiritual direction should be lost.

In Chapter I we noted that such older images of ministers as Master and Builder have declined. At one point the image of the minister as Pastoral Director was proposed as a new dominant understanding. We would understand the Pastoral Director today under the rubric of Reflective Practitioner, leaving open the possibility that the Reflective Practitioner might devote more time to teaching, spiritual direction, and leading in social action than to traditional pastoral and management functions. Where ministers are to concentrate their time should be decided by practical Christian thinking rather than by sociologically determined, theologically uncriticized expectations of the congregations. That thinking needs to be done in the churches. We do not presume to predict its outcome. What we do urge is that in order to encourage this process and to renew the church in its Christian integrity, the churches think of their leaders as Practical Theologians, thereby increasing the prospects of their becoming such. It is with this understanding of professional leadership of the church in mind that we make our proposals about theological education.

Chapter V

The Education of Practical Theologians

In Chapter IV, we suggested that the church requires a type of leadership that differs significantly from those discussed in Chapter I. If this new type of leadership is to have any power, it is crucial that the seminaries organize themselves so as to make a maximum contribution to the development of practical theologians.

Of course, there are many qualifications for leadership in the church to which the seminary can contribute little. Native endowments, nurture in the life of the church, experience in leadership, and assignment of office by the church all are important, perhaps more important than formal education. This is as it should be. No educational institution achieves its goals in abstraction from the whole life of those whom it educates. The public schools of our country are too often expected to make up for deficiencies in parental nurture and instruction. They do not succeed. Similarly, theological schools are too often expected to make up for deficiencies in the life of local congregations. They do not succeed either. Theological schools need to know what they are and what they can contribute to the total life of the church, and they should do this well. What curriculum will make this possible?

First, there is a close connection between the subject matter of courses in Bible and church history and the deepening, broadening, and clarifying of Christian identity that we have described in preceding chapters. But these courses have seldom been taught with this purpose in mind. Thus the first section of this chapter will discuss what this aspect of the curriculum would be if it were reconceived according to this goal.

In Chapter III we indicated that the church that needs leadership and that realizes its Christian identity for our time is a church for the world, for the poor, for all peoples, and for women. This means that Christian decisions today are decisions made in a global context. But even in the church, our habits of looking at issues continue to be parochial. Section 2, therefore, will examine how seminaries can effectively introduce the global perspective to their students.

In Section 3 we shall study the analysis and solution of problems in terms of Christian identity and the global context of the church's life. Although this is relevant to all members of the seminary faculty, we shall focus on the changes needed in theology and ethics to implement this proposal.

In Section 4, we shall turn to those topics that belong to curriculum discussions but do not fit readily into the first three sections or the later discussion of reflective practice.

Sections 1 through 4 describe subject matter pertinent to all church leaders. But seminaries generally are also mandated to prepare persons for the specific profession of the parish ministry, and so theological education in the reflective practice of the parish ministry will be the topic of Section 5.

1. *The Seminary's Contribution to Christian Identity*

Nearly all seminaries devote considerable attention to Bible and church history, which indicates that there is universal recognition that the Christian story is important to ministers. However, it is less clear just why the story is important, and this is reflected in the confusion as to just what the purpose of these basic courses is.

Inevitably, most of these historical materials are taught by graduates of academic programs that concentrate on critical methodology. The analysis of ancient documents can be an end in itself. Those who have studied in this way and found the investigation of the past fascinating are likely to want to draw their theological students into this world of lore and methodological rigor. They have found that common assumptions about the teaching of the Bible and the story of the church are often superficial or erroneous, and they know that ministers should not perpetuate error. Hence, there is an obvious value in communicating a more accurate knowledge of the materials to seminarians.

But this extension of the university mentality into the seminary produces tensions. The student must learn to preach from biblical texts as the authoritative word for the Christian community, and the detached and critical way in which the professor discusses them will only exacerbate the problem of doing so. The superior student will rise above the difficulty and find hermeneutical styles that are responsible to both the academic community and the church. But most students are not superior, and they need help in learning how to preach responsibly from these texts. It is too much to ask the professor of preaching to solve this problem. To leave it to the systematic theologian is also a recipe for failure. Most historians know that their students need something more from them.

Because the most obvious "something more," as already indicated, pertains to preaching, the problem is especially acute for biblical scholars. They are responsible for the texts from which the weekly message is proclaimed. Most of them are concerned with how this proclamation occurs, and accordingly, they introduce relevant hermeneutical discussion into their teaching. But the state of hermeneutical discussion among academics is complex and confused. The different options are expressions of different commitments in theology, ethics, literary criticism, or philosophy. Students may learn a hermeneutical theory from their biblical professors that is at odds with what they learn in systematic theology or in pastoral theology. Also, the academic guild, finding hermeneutics to be academically messy, tends to stress the more "objective" aspects of historical study.

In any case, from our point of view, a combination of objective history and hermeneutics is still inadequate. The roles of the Bible and church history in the church are by no means limited to preaching, important as that is. Preaching needs to be understood in the wider context of the life and identity of the church.

Our argument, now reiterated often, is that the church needs to know its story, its whole story, in order to know what it is. This story is about how God has acted in the world creatively and redemptively. It is first and foremost the story of Israel as this was focused and transmitted through Jesus Christ and the apostolic faith in him. But it has continued from the time of the apostles to the present. To say who we are as Christians is, finally, to tell that story. Therefore, all Christians need to know that story, and the church needs leaders who know it well and can help others to learn it. Thus, the Bible and church history are the base of theological education because they are where the church's future leaders learn who they are as Christians.

If this is the principal reason for teaching Bible and church history in seminary, the teaching should reflect its purpose. These courses should guide the students into discovering their inner history. This past should be taught as our collective memory. Because the memory by which we live is so important, reflection on what to teach and how to teach it is crucial. We thus propose three main points: (A) internal history should be critical; (B) it should be inclusive; and (C) it should move toward universality.

A. *Internal History Should Be Critical*

The danger of our proposal is obvious, as it could be interpreted as encouraging the precritical teaching of our story. First, the history might be taught as though the internal history of those who produced our scriptures and our propagandistic Protestant or denominational histories needed no correction. In fact, we now know that there are many errors and distortions in the inner histories by which Christians have lived in the past, and we can see the harm that they have caused. Much of the idealization of objectivity has been in reaction to these errors. Therefore we do not wish to encourage a return to precritical styles of historical thought in any way.

For the teaching of history in the seminary, what is important to the individual is to know who one really is, and for this knowledge, criticism of one's own perceptions and memories is essential. The church must also know what it really is, and for that knowledge, criticism of its perceptions and memories is equally essential. Every historical methodology that helps Christians to attain a more accurate knowledge of themselves is sorely needed.

We cannot, however, identify accuracy with objectivity. As Niebuhr so well pointed out, the patient's account of the restoration of sight through an operation will differ from the surgeon's account. But the difference does not mean that one is more accurate than the other. There may be errors in either account that the other can help correct. But one will be an inner history of receiving one's sight, and the other will be an account of what can be observed as an outsider. What the church seeks to learn from those who write external histories is how to recount more accurately its internal history—not how to detach itself from the memories that give it its identity.

Precisely because this history is so important to the church, the passion for accuracy should be intense. Far from feeling that distortion can be tolerated because it always has been, Christians must be committed to its correction. Their integrity is at stake—not merely as scholars but also as human beings.

The second form of precritical teaching that our recommendation might wrongly encourage is failing to recognize the faults of our heroes. Stories of saints and martyrs and also of denominational leaders too often accent the virtues of their subjects and ignore their vices and weaknesses. Presumably the goal is to provide models for Christian living or to make readers feel good about their denominational identity. On a larger scale, the church's actions that we must recognize as shameful are often left unmentioned, whereas its heroism and successes are exaggerated.

These are the distortions of inner history to which the teaching of national history is very likely to succumb. It is thought that only a positive picture of this history can lead to the desired identity. A peculiar greatness of Israel lay in its refusal to deceive itself about its own history. The Jewish scriptures record the sins and failures of even the greatest heroes. They record also the people's refusal to follow God at crucial points in their history. Yet no people have been more affected by their internal history than have the Jews. The Christian tendency to self-deception can be checked by the Jewish scriptures that Christians have appropriated. In any case, we are convinced that sentimental falsifications of our internal history are both untrue to that history and self-defeating if their purpose is to form Christian identity today. Our call for teaching the Bible and church history as internal history is as much for the sake of repentance for collective Christian sins as for joy in solidarity with those who have gone before in the faith.

B. *Internal History Should Be Inclusive*

Historians know that after they have selected a period and a general topic, the process of selection has just begun. For example, if one decides to write on the Italian Renaissance, one must still determine whether one will write a political history, an economic history, an intellectual history, an art history, a cultural history, a social history, or something else. Will one write on what a few leaders accomplished or on the life of ordinary people during the period?

To decide on an internal history does not settle all the questions for the teacher of Christian history. An internal history could emphasize institutional developments, doctrinal developments, the history of preaching or liturgy, the history of Christian art, or the history of personal spirituality or piety.

Presumably something of all of these will be included in a good seminary course. Allotments of time should be based on the importance of past events in church life both for understanding who we are and how we became what we have become and as resources for dealing with contemporary issues. Although much is left to the teacher's judgment, and much will change from decade to decade, even from year to year, we think there can be some consensus. First, church leaders need to be familiar with the forms of worship (and of church organization) that prevail in our several traditions and how they came to be. Second, they need to know the sources of the ideas and beliefs to which many Christians feel committed and to which people still turn as authoritative. Third, they need to understand those events that produced the divisions still existing in the church. Fourth, they need to know something about the history of how Christians have related to other faith communities, so as to understand the attitudes and prejudices that are still held today. Fifth, they need to know how Christianity spread from Palestine around the world and what forms it has taken in different places and cultural contexts. Sixth, they need to know some of the ways that Christianity has dealt with past crises, so as to have models for dealing with ours. There could be other items on the list. However, the point is only that the commitment to study Christian history as *our* story does provide some reason for a selection.

More important even than these desiderata to the recovery of our memories is the question of *whose* history, within the whole mass of Christians, we shall study. Is it sufficient to attend to the best known leaders and trace the history through them? Or should we be more concerned with ordinary Christians and what faith meant in their lives? Surely the latter cannot be ignored altogether.

In recent years the narrowness of the traditional selection for remembering has been pointed out more and more often. Our histories have neglected ethnic minority churches in our own nation. They have largely ignored Christianity outside the North Atlantic area. Furthermore, and perhaps most critical of all, they have ignored the contribution of women, who have usually constituted more than half of the active participants in its life. This neglect has been twofold. First, it has resulted from the focus on church leaders and the lack of interest in what was happening with the mass of Christian believers. Second, even when women rose to public leadership, their contributions were depreciated and largely ignored. Indeed, rereading the Bible and church history with this new awareness leads to a much greater visibility of women throughout, and going below the level of public leadership to the religious life of the people discloses an even more prominent role for women.

To reread history to ask what women were doing also highlights the ways in which men used their power in and through the church to suppress them. One thereby understands the background of the resistance to women's ordination even today, and so the problem of gender in the church's language takes on new urgency.

For external history a strong argument can be made that these distortions should be rectified. For internal history, the matter is more pressing. Consciously or unconsciously, the history we have internalized has taught us that men are the real agents of history in general, and of church history in particular. This in turn influences our expectations and our attitudes in ways that continue to work against the equality of women today. To correct and revise our memory is to alter the way we move into the future.

The task of rewriting history is a large one, but much work has already been done. There are materials available today that the teacher of church history can use to introduce a measure of balance. This is also a place where students can share in the reinterpretation and understand its importance to the present.

C. *Internal History Should Tend Toward Universality*

There is another type of question that, with respect to seminary curricula, arises from the recommendation that history be taught as internal history. The accentuation of identity through the story told in the Bible and church history can, and often does, lead to a particularism that subordinates universalism. For example, too often in Protestant seminaries the history of Judaism is taught only through New Testament times, the history of the Eastern church is taught only through the patristic period, and the history of Roman Catholicism is taught only through the Council of Trent. Sometimes the history of Protestantism is taught only as a European phenomenon and the American scene is viewed only through denominational eyes. Therefore, identity as a member of a particular denomination is exaggerated, or the tendency to think that only Protestants are the true heirs of the common biblical heritage is subtly, or not so subtly, communicated, even when it is never stated. Clearly, this is undesirable. The basic identity of leaders for the church should be as inclusive as possible.

To become inclusive, Christian identity must be rescued from its ancient and enduring definition as non-Jewish and indeed anti-Jewish. That means that the story of Jews and Christians after the time of Jesus must be combined into a single story. Christians will read that story in the light of the centrality of Jesus Christ, but that will not cause them to side with other Christians in their persecution of Jews. Rather, it may cause them to see that much of the meaning of Jesus Christ has been more faithfully preserved among Jesus' compatriots than in Gentile Christianity.

The expansion of Christian internal history to include segments of Christendom other than the Western Protestant one, and to include the history of the Jews, is a heavy demand on the historical faculties. It requires instructors to readjust their offerings and venture into areas in which they may not feel qualified. And such expansion is in conflict with available books.

Despite the difficulties, this expanded Christian internal history is possible. Most historians can familiarize themselves with additional material as it is needed. The main change will be in the understanding of the purpose for selecting certain materials and working through their implications. The challenge will be to attain accuracy while communicating with few details and often at a level of sweeping generalization.

To ask for more now would be a mistake. By trying to do too much, one could easily fail to accomplish what is possible. Nevertheless, it is instructive to consider again the ultimate goal. It is not that we would learn to think of *us* Christians and Jews *as opposed to* the rest of the world, or even of *us* Christians and Jews and Muslims *as opposed to* Hindus and Buddhists. The goal is that we experience our identity with all for whom Jesus died. That will require a continuing expansion of the internal history out of which we live.

There is a tension between this universality and the particular focus on God's work with those people who have recognized it and interpreted their collective life in relation to it. But in principle this tension is broken in Jesus Christ, even though there are many respects in which Christians have been as particularistic as any other community has. This particularism can be overcome only when Christians adopt as their internal history the whole story of God's creative and redemptive work in the world.

Whereas Christians have a common center in Jesus Christ, they differ in their location of the circumference. Our argument is that there

should be no fixed circumference at all. This implies that the study of
Bible and church history as sources for our internal history functions best
when it opens Christians to wider reaches of history. Through the biblical memory they will find themselves remembering also the sources of
biblical thinking in Persia, Babylon, Egypt, and Canaan. That larger
history will also become theirs. Through the study of the church fathers
they will find themselves remembering the Greek philosophers in such a
way that they too become part of Christian internal history. Through the
study of modern church history they may find themselves remembering
the rise of modern science and philosophy as well as the Enlightenment.
Through the study of the movement of modern global missions they may
be drawn into examining the great religious traditions of India and
China and on into dialogue with their living representatives. Thus Christians will come to remember also Gautama and Confucius as part of
their internal history.

2. The Global Context

Christian identity is important in itself. It is also important as a basis
for responding to the situation in which, individually and corporately,
Christians now find themselves. This situation has many dimensions. It
includes the personal situation of the lonely individual, the tensions that
are tearing apart so many families, the church's struggle to understand
itself and win the loyalty of others, the economic problems of every local
community, the difficulty of making sense of traditional Christian ideas
in a changed intellectual and cultural climate, and the problem of adapt-
ing traditional Christian mores and ethical teaching to new social contexts. The tendency is to approach these problems on their own terms.

The result of Christian's approaching local problems in their local
context is a failure of understanding. There are two reasons for this.
First, the local problems are manifestations of systems that extend far
beyond the locality. For instance, the breakdown of the family cannot be
reversed by working on individual families' apparent problems, important as this ministry is. It is bound up with much larger patterns of social
change. The problems of the intellectual credibility and relevance of
Christian teaching cannot be treated in narrow horizons, important as it
is to help individuals with their personal crises of faith. Rather, they
express historical movements of huge proportions. In sum, to view local
problems as separate from their larger context is to misunderstand them.
They need to be seen in a global context if they are to be realistically
understood.

Second, to treat local problems in their local context is to fail to
approach them as Christians. As Christians, our concern is with the indivisible salvation of the whole world. When we try to solve the problems

of those who are nearest at hand without remembering this larger context, we are always in danger of helping some persons at the expense of others. All too often this means helping white middle-class church members at the expense of the poor, ethnic minorities, and the Third World.

According to the images of the church that we propose as suitable expressions in our time of our corporate memory, the context in which our Christian identity is to be lived now is global. The church is in the world and for the world. Our account thus should make clear that the world in question is the actual world of suffering humanity, part of whose suffering comes from the abuse of the remainder of God's creation. Clearly, not every Christian will have an identical view of the most salient features of our global situation. There are many legitimate differences of judgment. But we cannot consider our internal history seriously without acknowledging that God's work is for the whole world. To minister at any place in the world without regard for how that ministry is related to God's comprehensive activity is insufficient and can work against rather than with God.

Thinking in a global context cannot be taken for granted. Most North American whites have little understanding of what is occurring among blacks in the United States. They have even less knowledge of the world beyond their borders. A central task of the church, therefore, is to widen the horizons within which life is understood. If the church's future leaders are to do this, the seminary needs to help them widen their own horizons. Exposure to key elements of the global reality is essential to theological education.

Most seminaries do something in this direction. Courses in ecumenics, world mission, and the history of religions often expand the horizon of understanding to a worldwide level. But they rarely provide an orientation to all the salient features of the global situation. Students who gain a sensitivity to the planet's critical needs are more likely to do so through extracurricular reading, conversation, special conferences, and perhaps chapel. If they do achieve an understanding of the global context, that is what matters. But if this is critical to Christian thinking in the decades ahead, seminaries should not leave this to chance. Serious assessment of the global crisis should become part of the seminary curriculum.

Although thus far very little of the thinking of churches in North America has been informed by a world context, there is one major source of hope. The World Council of Churches thinks globally because its members come from all over the world. The fact that most of the ecumenical Protestant denominations in North America belong to it provides an opportunity for a global perspective to enter their life. Unfortunately, little attention is paid to the World Council of Churches at any level of North American church life. This is true even of most seminaries. One valuable way of introducing ministerial students to the global context is to make them aware of the work of the World Council of Churches in such a way that as they become church leaders they will help relate the church at all levels to the ongoing world discussion.

But whereas sustained instruction is required along these lines, global consciousness is not likely to be produced by instruction alone. All of seminary education should be globalized through the presence of a multiethnic, multicultural student body and faculty. Visitors from other countries and from oppressed minorities within this country can help. Better still, students need to spend some time living with the poor, whether in North America or elsewhere. There is no substitute for experiencing poverty firsthand and understanding how it is engendered by structural forces. The shock of reentry to our affluent and wasteful society is likely to leave its mark on the way all questions are considered in the future, and the thinking that results will be more appropriate to Christian internal history.

The world consciousness that is today Christian consciousness should permeate the entire curriculum and not be relegated to only one of its parts. This will happen to the extent to which the faculty itself participates in it. Whereas it can be assumed that most of the faculty have had their identities at least partly shaped by the study of Bible and church history, no comparable assumption can be made with respect to their global consciousness. Accordingly, seminary faculties that recognize the importance of this horizon to ministry need self-consciously to consider their own formation. Sabbaticals in Third World countries and participation in World Council of Churches activities can be encouraged. Professors may be asked to write papers on their disciplines indicating in what ways these disciplines are parochially Western and how they would be affected by a global consciousness. The seminary can hold conferences for its church constituencies on important aspects of the global crisis and involve its faculty in their leadership. However it is done, it should be an intentional activity. The pressures of academic guilds work in a quite opposite direction, and faculty members respond chiefly to dominant pressures.

3. Practical Christian Thinking

The church leader should be a practical Christian thinker. That means that he or she should bring Christian identity to bear on the understanding of the situation confronted by the church and its members. We have argued that this is possible today only when the situation is viewed in a global context.

If one asks which disciplines in the present curriculum are the most closely related to practical Christian thinking, the answer would have to be theology and ethics. This section thus will focus on the transformation of theology and ethics into practical Christian thinking.

In view of what we said in earlier chapters about Christian identity, it cannot be the task of systematic theology to formulate a conceptual scheme that supersedes Christian internal history as a source for further Christian thinking. Practical Christian thinking approaches each new issue with all of the church's memories. These should not be filtered through any one formal statement of the beliefs to which these memories have given rise and which they support.

This does not prohibit the formulation of systematic theologies. Such formulations are valuable. But these efforts, like those that have gone into creeds and confessions, simply become additional parts of that memory by which we live and think. The effort to capture the meaning of that history and exhaust it in a formulation of the beliefs to which it gives rise at any time and place is misdirected. But much that is valuable and true can still be expressed in this way.

Similarly, when Christian ethics tries to substitute principles or norms for the total internal history, it displays a lack of understanding of what it is to be a Christian. Christians are not those who live from any specifiable norms or principles. They are those who live from a rich and complex memory centering in Jesus Christ. Neither that history nor its center can be captured in ethical teachings. But this does not invalidate the effort to state for the church in its present situation which norms and principles appear at this juncture to be the most relevant and convincing. We have dealt with this task by proposing images of the church. The church needs systematic thinkers, for it needs to clarify what it believes and how it acts in every generation. But the church's memory reminds us not to take them too seriously. A living Christian memory soon gives rise to new formulations.

The major task of theology and ethics is to encourage students to think globally as Christians about the issues of the day. To think *as Christians* is to think from the memory of the church. The church remembers many who have undertaken so to think in the past. The student can thus learn much by studying them in their successes and their failures, but this belongs to Christian internal history rather than to practical Christian thinking.

Professors certainly should introduce the student to the efforts that others have made and are making to think as Christians regarding recent questions. Even more important is for professors to model the practical Christian thinking that students need to learn to do. And still more important is to elicit such thinking from the students and to encourage self-critical reflection on it.

The separation of theology and ethics into two disciplines has often had harmful consequences. It has heightened disciplinary self-consciousness in both areas, so that at present many of the leaders of both fields are devoting much of their energy to formulating methodologies for their disciplines. A cynic may say that representatives of both fields have less and less to say and think more and more about how to say it. The major exceptions are to be found among black, liberation, and feminist theologians who have refused to observe these disciplinary boundaries.

It would be far better if the energy of both theologians and ethicists went into thinking about the many important issues confronting Christians. Although these disciplinary and methodological questions are not as prominent in introductory courses for seminarians as within the professional guilds, the professors' preoccupations inevitably also color their presentation to their students. But pastors gain nothing by attempting to determine when they are functioning as theologians and when as ethicists.

A second negative consequence of this division has been that disciplinary self-definition has led to the neglect by both disciplines of many of the most important questions. Ethicists have tended to gravitate more toward medical ethics than toward the threat to global survival, not because the problems are more important but because they are more amenable to treatment in the categories of that discipline. Theologians have had great difficulty responding to the challenge of black theology and liberation theology because the issues were not posed in the terms established for the discipline.

The church will be far better served if its seminaries realize that there are many urgent questions being posed to the church in our time and that we need faculty who will reflect on these questions as Christians. Some of them, such as how we should think about God, fall within the existing self-definition of ethics. But even with these apparently clear cases, the separation of the disciplines can be distorting. Reflection on God that is not informed by the global context of threatened catastrophe is not adequate. Reflection on nuclear war that does not reflect on how God is now creatively and redemptively at work in the world is not adequate. The separation of disciplines does not necessitate such inadequacy, but it encourages it. Christian thinkers indifferent to whether they are functioning as theologians or as ethicists can contribute more to theological education and serve as better guides and models for future church leaders. The need in the seminary is for practical Christian thinkers who can help students to become practical Christian thinkers.

Although theology and ethics as academic disciplines are in particular need of being transformed into practical Christian thinking, such thinking already goes on in other parts of the seminary curriculum. For example, practical issues regarding sexuality and family are more often treated now in courses in pastoral care and counseling than in theology and ethics. Work in practical Christian thinking will need to involve faculty now teaching in the arts of ministry as well as theologians and ethicists.

No topic is more important for practical Christian thinking today than the church's mission. In general terms that mission is to the world and to the oppressed. But what that actually means for a denomination or a local congregation has ceased to be readily evident. Those who have most confidence about missions today are usually those who have been least sensitive to the legitimate criticisms of past church missions. Those who have been prepared to confess the sins of the past typically lack conviction as to the church's present mission. As a result, denominations do many things under the heading of mission and service to the world, most of them good, but they have no unifying or energizing vision of their call. Increasingly, local congregations have become ends in themselves, ministering to the felt needs of their members. The global horizon of Christian mission thus has become ineffective.

Ironically, this has happened at a time when the planet's needs have reached a crescendo of urgency. Injustice and oppression are rampant. Present policies are destroying the environmental basis for future human life. The threat of a nuclear holocaust hangs over us all. It is a strange time to suppose that meeting the felt needs of middle-class church members is an adequate response to God's call!

The problem is not that contemporary Christians are incapable of hearing God's call. The problem is more that the church leaders are not mediating that call. Because they recognize the inadequacy and even the inappropriateness for the current situation of earlier forms of mission, they do not call vigorously for the renewal of those forms. The formulation of an adequate church response to present needs would require intensive thought, and the church lacks the organs for that kind of thinking. Its bureaucracies are established to implement programs for the missional priorities determined by others. The legislative bodies authorized to determine such priorities have no time or opportunity for thought. It is recognized that any serious proposals would inevitably be controversial, and most church leaders hope to avoid controversy.

Theological seminaries would seem to be a place for serious thought about the church's mission. But such thought falls outside the major disciplines. Theologians are preoccupied with methodological questions and general beliefs. Ethicists formulate principles. Professors of missions are supposed to give instruction on the church's past world mission. But reflection on what the church is now called to do is not expected of any of these disciplines. Abolition of disciplinary boundaries would be a first step toward liberating seminary faculties to consider the most important issues facing the church and to encourage students to do so as well. This can begin with the boundary between theology and ethics.

Thus far we have opposed the disciplinary separation of theology and ethics, the concern to clarify disciplinary parameters and methodology, and the effort to systematize either doctrine or ethics. We have

noted that work in other fields also belongs to practical Christian thinking. We have argued for concern for the church's mission in general and
in the whole range of specifics. What implications does this have for
curriculum?

One possible course would deal with the church's overall mission in
the final years of the twentieth century. Other courses could deal with
segments of this mission. Some of these would appear more conventional.
For example, one need of the church is to clarify its affirmations regarding God, Jesus, itself, and so forth. The church needs leaders who are
able to help it in this task. Another course might ask about the church's
mission to a society wracked by ethnic conflict. This could resemble a
conventional course on race relations, although the focus on mission
would shift the emphasis. A third course could ask about the church's
mission to the middle-class family in its current crisis. Some of what is
now done in courses in pastoral care would appear in such a course.

A seminary may well decide that certain features of the Christian
mission are so important that courses pertaining to them should be
required of all students. This is certainly legitimate. But there are many
urgent topics to be addressed, and there is little time available within the
seminary curriculum. Any effort to cover all the topics is doomed to
failure and frustration. What is most important is helping the minister to
become a practical Christian thinker by developing the habit of viewing
a situation globally and as a Christian.

The contrast with what is required in historical courses should be
clear. Because there the purpose is identifying formation, they should
provide satisfactory coverage even at the price of sweeping generalization. What is included and what is omitted will influence the self-
understanding of the next generation of Christian leaders. These leaders
need to be able to teach the story to others, but they do not need to
engage in historical research as their professors do. On the other hand,
the best way to learn how to analyze and deal with problems according
to this Christian identity is practice in doing it. Of course, it is necessary
for the curriculum to give a proper sense of the scope and range of the
issues that practical Christian thinkers should address. For example, if all
the courses discussed social ethical problems, the wrong message would
be communicated. In this respect there are analogies with the situation
in the teaching of history. But whereas from historians ministers need
the relevant overview, as practical Christian thinkers they must decide
on new policies and actions. It is the style of thinking, not the particular
conclusions, that the seminary can teach.

Much of the work in courses on practical Christian thinking will be
historical. To approach a contemporary problem as a Christian is to
handle it as that internal history requires. Hence, a study of the church's

internal history cannot be limited to the survey courses designed to clarify and deepen Christian identity. It will take place in courses on practical Christian thinking as well. The difference will be that in the courses on practical Christian thinking specific questions will be addressed to the past. This leads to highly selective attention to the past.

Whereas the basic courses in history are likely to be taught best in traditional lectures, at least part of the education of the practical Christian thinker will require projects by students that should be critically evaluated by the class. Case studies may be useful as well. This does not exclude extensive lecturing as long as the lectures are devoted to modeling the needed practical Christian thinking.

4. Neglected Topics

The preceding proposals are an effort to give rationale and direction to the major goals of the seminary curriculum. Apart from preparation for reflective practice, to which we will come later, they envision the core of education for practical theologians. But they do not exhaust the needed curriculum. There are many concerns now directed to the seminaries that they do not clearly address. And although theological schools should avoid trying to correct every weakness among ministers by providing additional courses, some of these concerns are important. We shall discuss five important topics to which we are directed by these concerns: (1) other religious traditions, (2) the sociology, psychology, and philosophy of religion, (3) the arts and the mass media, (4) spiritual disciplines, and (5) denominational studies.

First, would the study of religious traditions other than Judaism and Christianity lose even the precarious foothold it now has in some seminary curricula? Other religious traditions are obviously not central to Christian internal history. They are present in the global scene, but if they are studied only for their relation to the most salient features of that scene, they may be viewed only sociologically. Their existence raises some practical problems for Christianity today, for example, in relation to the continuation of traditional missions to non-Christians. But practical Christian thinking in the seminary can treat only a few of the practical problems facing the church.

Is there, then, a case for studying other religious traditions as part of the core of seminary education understood as the preparation of practical Christian thinkers? We believe that there is and that it relates to all three of the above areas. The world today contains vital traditions other than Christianity. Many contemporary Christians come from cultures shaped by these religious traditions and cannot establish their own Christian identity well without incorporating their contributions. Globally the problem of indigenizing Christianity in many cultures is a critical one.

Even within North America this problem is important, and all of us live in a culture to which a plurality of religious traditions are contributing. Christian identity needs to incorporate this plurality.

Furthermore, Christian identity becomes clear today only as it is compared with other possible identities. If this comparison is made only through the eyes of Christians of earlier times, it will be distorted. Christians must repent their sins in this regard. They can hardly form the new identity of repentance if they know of other religious identities only vaguely. The study of other attractive religious identities, therefore, is essential to shaping a healthy Christian identity today.

For understanding the global reality, also, the importance of studying other religious traditions is greater than it first appears. On the whole, these, like Christianity, appear to be in decline as forces directly influencing national life and policy, although Islam may be an exception. But Christians know that their post-Christian culture cannot be understood apart from its Christian roots, and that even today authentic Christian faith plays a role too easily ignored by sociologists. The same is true of Buddhism in post-Buddhist cultures and of Hinduism in post-Hindu cultures. A theological school should not underestimate the power of religious commitments in our modern secular world!

Finally, practical Christian thinking cannot regard the existence of other religious traditions as simply one of many interesting topics. The fact that other traditions exist alters the character and content of all responsible Christian thinking. The consciousness of such pluralism already has changed the way in which most Christian theology is transmitted. But too often the awareness of pluralism is abstract; too often it leads to a false relativization of Christian theology that deeper engagement could avoid. Healthy Christian thinking therefore requires encounter with other religious traditions.

A case could, therefore, be made for locating the teaching of other religious traditions in any of the above three sections or by itself as a separate area. Our recommendation is that it be included in the third section—practical Christian thinking. This would lead to its being taught differently than it is in colleges and graduate schools. It would be taught for Christians as a challenge and opportunity for Christian thinking and self-understanding. This would be possible only if the other tradition were presented as the attractive option for Christians that it in fact is. But the course would also show how Christians have responded and how they should now respond. What changes in Christian self-understanding and doctrine are called for in light of what one learns from other traditions? How does this affect the Christian mission? These questions are now being asked by many theologians, and they need to be introduced more thematically into the education of church leaders.

Second, no place is provided in this scheme for the social sciences, including the sociology and psychology of religion. This does not mean that sociology and psychology have not influenced our proposals. The type of historical study recommended has strong sociological elements. Both sociology and psychology have much to contribute to resolving many of the issues facing the church today. As we move on to the specifically professional features of the curriculum, the importance of sociology and psychology will continue to be apparent.

In the past it was often felt that if any discipline could contribute to the curriculum, it needed to be represented by a course. Because ministers cannot deal intelligently with the problems that face them and the church without understanding matters sociologically and psychologically, it is thereby supposed they must be introduced to the disciplines of sociology and psychology.

It is this kind of thinking that we are opposing. We have argued against introducing students to the *disciplines* of theology and ethics, not because Christians do not need to think theologically and ethically, but because to think theologically and ethically requires practice in thinking that way rather than knowledge of those disciplines. The same is true of thinking sociologically and psychologically. When a course covers problems that have obvious sociological and psychological aspects—and what problems do not?—these aspects must be examined. But that is quite different from requiring introductory courses in the sociology and psychology of religion. Often the connection between what is learned in such courses and the questions that arise in practical Christian thinking is minimal.

Our answer is that we do not favor including courses in sociology and psychology as such. But there is another question. Does a faculty need a sociologist or a psychologist or both? Here the answer is different. At the least, a faculty needs persons who are sufficiently sensitive to the issues treated in these disciplines to help the other faculty members and students think intelligently about the problems raised by the real world.

There is little danger that the sociological and psychological aspects of questions will be ignored, as they dominate many discussions in our culture. But there is a danger that seminary faculty and students will use outdated notions in these areas and arrive at superficial conclusions unless there are colleagues who are well versed in the literature and can interpret the significance of empirical and clinical studies.

The philosophy of religion also disappears from this curriculum. Here, too, we believe that as a separate discipline it has distracted from what is needed for church leadership as much as it has contributed. But it has also offered much that the seminary cannot afford to lose.

The philosophy of religion has kept in focus Christians' implicit claim that what they say makes sense and is true. It has pressed for clarity and justification, whereas theology often hides its confusion behind familiar rhetoric. In some of its forms it has judged among competing Christian formulations or even established new ones. All of these are important services.

Unlike sociology and psychology, current philosophy does not provide categories of thought that have become common sense in our culture. Hence there is no assurance that faculty and students will be attentive to the philosophical dimensions of the problems they face. It often requires considerable probing to bring thought to the level at which philosophy's importance appears.

For these reasons, although we oppose a separate course in philosophy of religion, we find it even more necessary here than in psychology and sociology that there be members of the faculty who can explain problems' philosophical dimensions and propose solutions. This will be particularly difficult without a context for sustained philsophical study, but the effort must be made.

A third area, already slighted in most seminaries, is the arts. There is nothing in our discussion above to exclude them, and there is no better way of understanding our internal history than by studying the history of Christian art. But in fact few church historians are well equipped to teach Christian art. Artists speak powerfully about the present situation and the need for a Christian response. But there is too great a likelihood that practical Christian thinkers also will neglect this resouce. There is a danger that many ministers will graduate from the curriculum we propose—as at present—poorly prepared to enjoy and profit from the arts and to use them effectively in church life. We have proposed nothing that will do much to heal the breach between modern Protestant church life and the community of artists.

More is at stake for the church in this than a general enrichment of life and understanding for church leaders. The church cannot bring wholeness to human life when it neglects the dimension of imagination. We all live by images as much or more than by concepts, and it is the arts that are mainly responsible for generating images and making them effective. Rational, discursive language separated from such images fails to touch the deepest springs of emotion and motivation. The church needs the arts.

It is equally true that imagination cut off from rational analysis and criticism is untrustworthy and even dangerous. The arts need reason as much as reason needs the arts. To neglect them is to contribute to the growing sickness of our divided culture and our divided selves. At least at the rational, discursive level this topic can be treated both by understanding the Protestant heritage from the Reformation and the Enlightenment and by identifying the problem for consideration in practical Christian thinking. But we know that a discursive treatment of the arts does not go far to integrate the aesthetic and rational ways of experiencing the world.

We should say frankly that we have no short-term solution for this problem. To require courses in the arts is an ad hoc, stopgap measure that may be necessary but does not really resolve the problem. What is needed, rather, is a reeducation of the community so that the arts will cease to be segregated from the discursive mode that dominates education. That will not happen unless there are within the community those who will aggressively press the arts on the collective attention.

Although we do not belittle the value of introducing the arts into the curriculum, even in a segregated fashion, we believe that it should be the whole community's concern to encourage their presence in all aspects of its life. Community worship is one place. The campus itself provides a locus and a context for reflection on the aesthetic dimension of life. Extracurricular artistic activities should be given high priority by the administration and faculty. In time, the presence of the arts in the community may increase attention to them in all the curriculum's courses. However, this is not likely to go far without the conscious commitment of the faculty.

Whereas in our society it becomes more and more possible to be isolated from the community of serious artists and their work, the mass media affect all of us. In this case there is no question of the seminary's being untouched. But there is the likelihood that there will be too little reflection on how all are being influenced.

One response, of course, is to require a course on this subject. Such a course can certainly be valuable. But the addition of courses on topics of this kind carries schools back into the problems of proliferation that have so confused them in the recent past.

Another alternative is to be aware of how the mass media affect both the global situation and the problems confronted by the church. For example, the distortions of the situation in Central America by the mass media, especially as they are influenced by the government, are essential to any discussion of the Christian mission related to that region. The presentation of adolescent sexuality in the media requires the attention of any who would minister to adolescents. The image of women in the media is of obvious importance as seminaries deal with the question of the church for women. What is needed more, therefore, than specialized courses is reflection on how the media enter into all the problems of our society and on how they might be used positively. Until such reflection becomes a part of scholars' habits, the faculty needs to include those who will remind them of this dimension of their shared lives and who will be able to guide those willing to expand their analysis of the situation.

There is another role for the electronic media in theological education. Because they are indeed the media of our day, it is necessary that church leaders be able to use them. This use should not be disconnected from the other relationships of the arts and media to theological education. To use them well requires a sensitivity to the visual and auditory arts that we do too little to cultivate. But the church cannot wait for the development of artistic sensibilities and gifts before learning to use the major means of contemporary communication. Although there are other, more effective ways to communicate with television, it can be used simply to record the sorts of things the church is already doing. While the church moves slowly toward finer things, it would be wise to use television even in the simplest ways.

We suggest, therefore, that seminaries should at least expose their students to televising services of worship and to preaching on television. Using videotapes for educational purposes and producing them inexpensively within and for the church opens up other points of contact between the arts of ministry and the world of media. Perhaps out of such beginnings, the ability to bring the gospel effectively to masses of people will be found. Until this happens, it is likely that the church's voice will grow weaker.

Fourth, there has recently been a ground swell of attention to the seminary's responsibility to minister to its students' spiritual needs and to guide them into personal disciplines that will strengthen them in their Christian life. Since the demise of pietism, there has been no consensus as to how to nurture Christian commitment, conviction, and fervor, especially of those who lead the church. Some who believe they have found ways to do this seek the seminary's cooperation, but more often the church turns to the seminary out of confusion, seeking help.

This current interest is often called spirituality and spiritual disciplines. This is unfortunate, because the connotations of the Latin word *spiritualitas* are otherworldly and individualistic. These connotations continue to affect expectations and experiments. There is a tendency to focus on states of consciousness and their psychological effects. The exploration of these is open to Christians, and there are opportunities to learn from the ancient traditions of India and China. But this cannot constitute the heart of the seminary's responsibility for the Christian formation of students.

The more common term in recent Protestantism was the *devotional life*. This was much used in later pietism, and it is better than spirituality in that it has a clearer relational element. The Christian is devoted to God and to participating in God's creative and redemptive work in the world. But when devotion becomes lukewarm, authentic Christian living gives way to formalism and legalism. Christians know the dangers of this loss of devotion and try to order their lives so that it will be constantly renewed. The practices through which devotion is renewed can be called the *devotional life*.

The danger of emphasizing the devotional life used to be that the practices designed to enhance devotion sometimes became ends in themselves. Reading the Bible, praying alone, and attending prayer meetings came to be in themselves the embodiment of devotion rather than ways to nurture it. The devotional life thus could be substituted for devoted living; authentic piety thus became pietism.

The seminary needs both to share the authentic concerns that lead to the call for spirituality and to refuse to support the distortions of Christian faith to which spirituality or the devotional life can so easily lead. Perhaps it can do this by changing these terms to discipleship. Even that can too easily be interpreted as being individualistic, but it has the advantage of being clearly biblical and referring to the active expression of faith in the whole of life, inner and outer, rather than to limited aspects. By concentrating on images of the church in Chapter III we hoped to set discipleship into the corporate context where it belongs.

In contributing to the education of the church's leaders, the seminary has the opportunity and responsibility to contribute to the understanding and practice of discipleship. This includes a concern for deepening and clarifying the commitment to discipleship in ways that neither the scholarly study of subject matters nor the training in skills has done. We hope and believe that an education based on Christian identity, global consciousness, and practical Christian thinking will be much more directly related to Christian discipleship. Ideally, much of the legitimate criticism of the seminaries' spiritual aridity will be dissipated when the curriculum is reordered to promote discipleship.

The central Christian practice for deepening and clarifying the commitment to discipleship has always been corporate worship. This, too, has an important place in the seminary. Of course, such worship can be turned by some into the *embodiment* of discipleship, but most of the church's historic liturgy works against that. The study of worship belongs in the seminary curriculum also, as a theme in the study of our history and in the education of the reflective practitioner, of which we will be speaking soon.

Christians have always been encouraged to supplement corporate worship with private prayer and mutual sharing. In addition, the seminaries should provide opportunities for small groups to gather for mutual encouragement in discipleship. The prayer and sharing central to worship also provide norms for this private prayer and small group sharing. These norms are needed, as there is nothing necessarily Christian about prayer and sharing. They can work just as easily against discipleship as for it, leading to complacency rather than to solidarity with the poor.

But what does this mean for the curriculum? It certainly means that reflection on Christian discipleship and its nurture should be included in it. A curriculum that generally discourages such reflection should certainly add a course dealing with this. No subject matter could be more important. But two caveats are in order.

If special courses are added, it is better that they be inclusively on

Christian discipleship rather than on spirituality. As we have indicated, a concentration on spirituality separated from the context of discipleship is likely to lead to narrow definitions of spirituality.

But when dealing with such lacunae of theological education, even one as important as this, adding courses cannot solve the problem. Christian discipleship and the spirituality that supports it should not be treated apart from the Bible, church history, the global context, and practical Christian thinking. Separated from the rest of the curriculum, such study encourages the separation of discipleship and especially spirituality from the rest of thought and life. If the course attempts instead to systematize the results of past Christian experience for the present, it will fare no better than have similar undertakings in theology and ethics. We prefer to have the commitment to discipleship structure the entire curriculum. Specific questions about Christian discipleship, including those about spiritual disciplines, should be answered in the context of practical Christian thinking.

Fifth, in recent years we have seen an increase of attention to denominational requirements. These have expressed diverse concerns. One has been that seminary graduates did not have a sufficient denominational identity to remain loyal to the program of a denomination and to accept its disciplines. This concern is legitimate but dangerous. The primary identity that the seminary should address is Christian identity. To show that this Christian identity is especially well expressed in a particular denominational identity can only reinforce the fragmentation of Christendom. On the other hand, to form a denominational identity that supersedes the Christian identity falsifies the nature of both. If a denominational identity can be established as one form of Christian identity among others, and one that is in principle ecumenically committed, it is harmless; and if this enables ministers to function better within the existing institutions and to make their contributions within the ecumenical movement, it is healthy.

The question is how a healthy denominational identity should be formed. The present trend is toward a segregated segment of the seminary curriculum committed to this task. But this seems to teach just the wrong identity, if it succeeds at all. Often the segregated courses are among the least interesting in the curriculum, communicating a legalistic demand of the denomination rather than a sense of belonging. Taking these courses can be a test of denominational loyalty rather than a means of instilling it.

The reasons for requiring denominational courses may, of course, be of a different sort. It may be held, for example, that in order to work in a church of a particular denomination, one must be familiar with its polity, doctrine, history, liturgy. There is no doubt that some practical information is needed. The problem, however, with this approach—a problem that arises whenever the approach to education is a list of all the things the program's graduates should know—is that the list will expand indefinitely. It is difficult to declare that any part is not necessary. But the result of packing information into a set of required courses is dull courses whose content will not be remembered long. Too, a nationally determined course syllabus is unlikely to inspire exciting teachers.

Denominations have a legitimate interest as the future employers of seminary students in the way their history, doctrine, and polity are taught. But the seminaries, in their eagerness to garner denominational support, have too quickly agreed to denominational requirements. They should ask that the goals be spelled out and propose working together to find means of meeting them. If these goals are socialization into the denomination and sufficient information about its history and ways of operation to enable the minister to function effectively in the existing institution, they can be better attained by incorporating denominational studies into the broader seminary curriculum, by supervised experience in the church, and by extracurricular activities on the seminary campuses.

The incorporation of denominational concerns into the general curriculum must not be casual. The history of the denomination and its distinctive teaching must be dealt with seriously in the context of the larger history of the church and especially of the church in North America. If the student body is multidenominational, time must be allotted for students individually or in denominational groups to study their history and receive help from their professors. In the study of the church, students must investigate the problems and potentials of the polity in which they plan to work. They will understand this better when they become aware of the alternatives. Similarly, in the study of worship, it is important to understand one's own tradition as one among others, but specifically as one's own.

Also some of the topics covered in practical Christian thinking will require denominational self-consciousness. For example, the current debates about the ordination of homosexuals include both the theoretical meaning of ordination and its practical efforts, which differ among denominations. When ordination guarantees an appointment, issues arise that are not present when it follows upon a call. Pastors as practical Christian thinkers therefore must be able to handle the particular problems of their own denominations, and their study of practical Christian thinking should help them do this.

5. *Professional Education for Parish Ministry*

Thus far we have considered the curriculum as it affects Christian identity, clarifies the context within which Christians live, and helps the students develop practical Christian thinking. All of these are appropriate for leaders in the Christian community, whether they are clerical or lay, closely related to local congregations or operating in church bureaucracies and other capacities. In fact, theological schools provide programs for persons who will use their education in a variety of professional settings. This should certainly continue when the schools' resources allow it. But at this point, we shall turn to the seminaries' primary task, the education of practical theologians who will be ministers in local congregations. Though some of the educational opportunities described in this section would be helpful to church leadership in general, our attention will be directed to the education of these ministers and the way in which the seminary can help meet their needs most effectively.

Faculty members who are closest to these concerns are likely to be those whose fields are in the so-called practical side of the curriculum, including the psychology of religion and the sociology of religion. As we noted earlier, it was the radical disjuncture between the "theory," represented by the so-called academic disciplines in the theological schools, and the institutions' demands on the professionals that led to expanding the practical disciplines in the theological school curriculum. By introducing sociology and psychology as a new theory base, educators thought they could enable graduates to become better congregational leaders. But the problem, as we have shown, was not simply with the type of theory. Rather, it is with the modern professional paradigm, which insists that theory and practice can be neatly divided. Unfortunately, the so-called practical fields in the theological schools have fallen into the disciplinary trap as well. More often than not, the classes in Christian education, pastoral counseling, and church management focus on the "theory" of the emerging discipline as much as they do on critical thinking about practice in the congregation. They thus accentuate the influence of the modern professional paradigm in the seminary's curriculum.

Our proposals reject this model for professional education in general and for professional theological education in particular. We have adopted from Schoen the idea of the reflective practitioner, agreeing with him that in the actual work of most professionals, application of theory plays a minor role. This is, of course, the old idea of learning by doing, combined with the awareness that all practice is laden with theory and that the professional needs to be able to recognize the theory implicit in the practice, to develop it in the light of the practice, and to improve the practice in relation to the improved theory. We also realize that the real understanding of the skilled professional remains partly implicit or tacit.

Shoen has suggested that much of what is needed for reflective practice must be learned on the spot. Reflective practice requires reflection on the actual practice of professionals in their institutional locations. Because the seminary is not the institutional location for pastoral ministry, much of the learning that arises from and prepares one for reflective practice in ministry must be done in the churches themselves.

A. *The Role of the Churches in Professional Education for Ministry*

Theological educators have long recognized professional ministers' need for educational opportunities that placed them in actual practice in a church and gave them some supervision and chance for reflection on their practice with other practitioners. There have been a variety of attempts to meet those needs.

The earliest attempt to provide some sort of experienced-based teaching was the addition of full-time or part-time faculty members recruited from those in professional practice in congregations. However, ministerial practitioners brought to seminary faculties are seldom accorded the same status as faculty members are whose fields fit more aptly the model of modern university specialties. Moreover, it is difficult for practitioners removed from regular practice to remain in touch with their own work. Usually, they quickly turn from offering opportunities for reflection in action to some form of research-based reflection *on* action.

Another attempt to provide experienced-based instruction has been, instead, to move the students to the practitioner's institutional location. Students have been sent to observe practitioners as they practiced and to participate in reflective practice with the more experienced professionals. Loosely referred to as *field education*, these educational devices were implemented by the seminaries through field placements in part-time positions and in full-time internships. Both devices were attempts to replicate, to some degree, the medical internship in theological education.

Part-time field placements have not been especially helpful in providing the kinds of learning opportunities required for reflective practice. Students tend to view these placements as jobs to supplement their income, and churches see the placements as inexpensive, part-time staffing. The supervision, for the most part, is haphazard, and there is little systematic reflective conversation in the midst of practice or even at the seminary. The students' responsibility is usually confined to work with youth and children, and there is very little opportunity for participation in, or even observation of, counseling by the experienced professional supervisor.

Full-time internships do, by and large, offer more valuable learning opportunities. In the best of these internships, reflection and action take place under the supervision of an experienced professional who is prepared to give immediate feedback to the student intern. Yet, even the best of these experiences are often isolated from the rest of the seminary curriculum, so that they are little more than interludes and not an integral part of the curriculum. Few of the faculty directly supervise the interns, and most of the faculty have little or no interest in the matter. Usually it is only the field education supervisors who receive reports on these experiences, and their supervision is minimal. Moreover, their appointment is most often administrative, and it is only rarely that they are accorded full faculty status on the basis of their field education supervisory responsibilities alone. Thus, it is hardly surprising that field education is tangential to most of the regular curriculum, even in the practical fields.

There are a few impressive field education programs, but in the main, they are expensive and difficult to sustain. Such programs seem to us to be beyond the capability of most of the theological schools. We, therefore, propose that the churches assume the major responsibility for education in reflective practice. How this will be done will depend on many factors and must be decided by those persons in the churches who will be responsible for implementing the proposals. However, we do venture a proposal, one that in our view would be very effective.

We suggest that after graduation from the seminary, ministers be given the status of probationary ordinands. They would be placed in teaching congregations selected for participation in an educational program in cooperation with the area's theological schools. The selection of the congregations would be the responsibility of the various denominations, and the regional judicatories would be responsible for recruiting and training the leadership and organizing the educational program. Probationers would be assigned pastoral responsibilities and would be compensated for their work. They would work closely with a teaching pastor who, along with lay leaders, would talk with the probationers about their effectiveness. They would also talk with the probationers about the theological grounding of their ministry and the theological bases for certain functions and priorities in the church.

The teaching congregations might be organized cooperatively into regional or metropolitan clusters in which ongoing reflection on practice could be shared among several probationers and their supervisors, in periodic seminars and in conference settings. The seminary faculty should be invited into these sessions, both to learn from them and to contribute to them.

The churches would decide on the length of the probationary experience. One year would be a minimum; two would be desirable. Or the period might be determined by the supervisor's judgment as to the individual probationer's readiness for ministry. In any case, full ordination would follow this period of supervised reflective practice. It is hoped that the habit of reflective practice developed during this period would continue during the remainder of the new minister's professional career.

This proposal, obviously, is analogous to normal practice in medicine. Graduates of medical schools intern in teaching hospitals where they receive minimum compensation and close supervision. The emphasis in our case, however, falls heavily on reflection about practice. This is not only a reflection on the practical aspect of how well one is doing according to what is required in all professions; it is also a theological reflection. The modes of reflection developed in practical Christian thinking in the seminary should be used to analyze the problems that will arise in professional practice in the church. The seminary and the church will need to work together to see that this happens. Professionalism must not be allowed to supersede Christian identity, the global context, and the practical thinking informed by these.

B. *The Seminary's Contributions to Education for Reflective Practice*

If the churches accepted our proposal, the seminaries would no longer be responsible for what has traditionally been called field education. Reflective practice in ministry would be taught at the institutional location of pastoral practice under the supervision of practicing ministers. We believe that this is where church management, polity, and general pastoral care can best be taught. This does not mean that the seminary should ignore reflective practice. Indeed, the seminary faculty should be very much involved in the teaching congregations that we have proposed. They would not be asked to be experts in the practice of ministry nor would they be expected to serve as field supervisors. Rather, they would be expected to do those things they can do well. In light of this, it seems reasonable to expect that a larger and more representative group of seminary faculty would become involved in education for reflective practice. It is also conceivable that continuing education for practicing ministers could be correlated with the instruction of probationary ordinands. If this were done, the demands on the seminary faculty and teaching pastors created by the new organization of education for reflective practice would not be viewed as an additional burden but, rather, as a more creative recasting of current responsibilities.

Beyond their support of and participation in the teaching congregations, the seminary faculties may contribute to education for reflective practice in their own institutional settings.

(1) Reflection on the congregational context of ministry. One important seminary contribution to reflective practice will be the provision of opportunities for students to study the congregation. Since the congregation is the institutional location for the practice of pastoral ministry, it is crucial for ministers to know something about the way in which they function institutionally and how they are related to their unique social locations. While many ministers do intuit the "sense" or "spirit" of a congregation and are able to operate effectively on that basis, even these gifted individuals can benefit from a more systematic

understanding of their context.

Obviously, the study of the congregations at the seminary will not be based on direct observation by all the students themselves. What the seminary can do, however, is introduce students to a variety of approaches to the study of the congregation. This will equip students with the background necessary to do what Schoen has called "frame analysis," the examination of the specific context of professional practice on a case by case basis.

The approaches which most readily come to mind are sociological, psychological, and theological.[1] From a sociological perspective, students may learn to recognize the significance of the social location of a particular congregation, and the ways in which its social setting affects its self-understanding. Moreover, it is possible to discern the patterns of inter-action between members of the congregation which shape the process of formal decision-making and determine the formal allocation of power among individuals.

A psychological approach to the study of the congregation may yield a more adequate understanding of the dynamics of group behavior and the causes of interpersonal conflict between the members of the congregation, particularly as those conflicts emerge in the ongoing life of the congregation itself.

Much of the responsibility for this kind of study will be borne by faculty members in the so-called "practical" fields, since they are more likely to have substantial backgrounds in the social sciences than those in other disciplines in the theological schools. Yet here, as in other parts of the curriculum, there can be no sharp disciplinary lines. The key perspective from which the congregation is to be viewed is theological, and that perspective is informed by the participation of everyone who teaches in the school. What the congregation is, sociologically and psychologically, must always be put in the context of the historically formed identity of the church and a conception of what the congregation is and ought to be in its present concrete world historical situation. The congregation is the church. As such it cannot be understood apart from reflection on its mission and purpose.

(2) Reflections on models of practice. Another important contribution which the seminary has often made to reflective practice is the provision of opportunities for reflection on models of practice. A great amount of research has been done on the various patterns of practice in the church and the problems attending them. We have in mind especially pastoral counseling, church management, and religious education.

---

[1] Cf. Carl Dudley, ed., *Building Effective Ministry* (San Francisco: Harper & Row, 1983).

The presentation of the materials in the seminary courses should include attention to models drawn from other professions. There is a certain commonality in the work of managers, teachers, and counselors wherever they serve; hence the minister as one who manages, teaches, and counsels can take advantage of research on these functions in other professional settings. But this does not suffice. Researching the models for practice of ministry must be focused on the specific task of pastoral leadership in the congregation. This means that the reflection will include some critical examination of the various possible models of management and counseling from the perspective of Christian identity and practice. Christian practice in the profession of ministry is certainly no less the practice of Christian ministry in the world than is the ordinary practice of serious Christians in general. As such, it must be a manifestation of who ministers are as Christians in their particular social location.

Classroom experience of this sort can extend the options for professional action in ministry. In fact, some reflection on professional action which is characterized by clear reference to research on models of action is absolutely necessary if we are to move beyond highly personal intuitive responses to situations. To some degree, each situation confronting the professional is unique, and the personal response of any professional will differ from that of another in a similar situation. Yet no one can deny the advantage of sharing systematic reflective insight on professional experience. There are relevant similarities among congregations which are as significant as their differences. This means that it is possible to observe and share certain patterns of practice which will assist aspiring professionals in their quest for greater competence in the functions expected of them by every congregation.

Much of what has been suggested here is already included in seminary courses listed under religious education, pastoral counseling, and church management. Yet there is a great deal of repetition in the teaching of those courses. Models of group behavior are important to all of these functional tasks. Patterns of teaching and learning are critical for all of them, and no one can function as a manager, counselor, or director of education without some understanding of personality dynamics and personality development. Theological criticism of anthropological assumptions and relational patterns is necessary in every case. Imaginative reorganization of present course offerings could eliminate much duplication, and at the same time provide more of the needed presentation of models of practice for the reflective practitioner.

(3) *Contextual education.* We have already argued that the churches have the main responsibility for educating their pastoral leaders for reflection in action. Yet what they learn at the seminary must be closely

related to what they learn in the church. We believe that this relationship should begin during the first year of theological studies, with some exposure to church life and ministry under the guidance of ministers and lay persons as well as faculty. What we have in mind is not reintroducing field education but combining students' part-time positions in churches with their seminary course work.

One of the best ways that this may be done at the seminary is by developing what have come to be called *contextual* components in courses of instruction. By this we mean that certain designated courses in the curriculum should include the requirement that students participate in congregations as part-time paid or unpaid practitioners. What the students experience in the church and what they learn in the classroom should be integrated in such a way that there is clarity about the relationship between actual practice and reflection on models of practice and on the context of practice.

There have been many experiments in seminaries along these lines. In some cases, courses from the seminary have been taken to nearby congregational locations where laity, students, and ministers all teach and learn together. In other settings, alternative systems of theological education have been devised which were focused on actual practice in the congregations as the primary reference point for all seminary teaching. *All* courses consisted of reflection *on* actions of the students as they practiced ministry. There have also been a considerable number of experiments with extension models of reflective practice in which the students' congregational bases were widely scattered, and courses of instruction simply brought the students together periodically for reflection.

None of these experiments have proved to be satisfactory. Alternative congregationally-based education, and education by extension, do indeed enlarge the opportunity for reflection in action, but they sacrifice the immense value of seminary-based practical reflection on professional action, particularly the kind of reflection which must be based on continuing biblical, historical, and social-scientific research. The congregation simply does not provide the setting, time, or resources for the disciplined study required for professionals who will lead the Christian community in its search for an adequate contemporary expression of its identity along with reflection on authentic concrete Christian practices in its world-historical context.

Simply taking seminary courses to the congregation does not, in itself, change anything. One could simply duplicate the same courses in another setting, which is what happens more often than not.

From our point of view, therefore, the only promising experiments are those that introduce contextual components into courses taught at the seminary. In one experiment at Claremont, students in a class are assigned to work for limited periods of time in "teaching congregations" under the supervision of selected pastors. In the same course, there is classroom instruction of the sort described in the previous sections. Models of practice, theories of action, and perspectives on the congregation are presented. These presentations are supplemented by seminar sessions involving the teaching pastors and the seminary faculty. In the seminar sessions, there is a very serious attempt at integrating the reflection *on* action of the classroom presentations with the reflection *in* action experienced by the students under the direction of the teaching pastors. This sort of pedagogy intentionally seeks to exhibit integrative action/ reflection which at once expands the knowledge of models and context for students and exhibits the kind of immediate flexible response required of a professional responding to unique and changing situations of practice.

At the present time, most of the experiments in contextual education courses pertain to subject matter traditionally included in arts of ministry courses. These courses are attempts to overcome the problems we have pointed to in field education and field placement. We have insisted all along that the entire curriculum must be one for practical theologians. But if the organization, pedagogy, and content of the so-called academic courses remain the same, even these contextual experiences will not be effective. If, however, there are moves in the directions we have suggested for the curriculum as a whole, then these experiments in contextual education may be able to join practical thinking and reflective practice. In a curriculum consisting of courses educating practical theologians, there is surely room for more creative experimentation along these lines.

(4) Opportunities for reflective practice in the seminary. Contextual education is not the only way in which the seminary may prepare students in reflective practice. Some pastoral functions can be simulated within the school or in other institutional settings, and instruction there has proved to be helpful. For example, simulated preaching with immediate feedback in the classroom has long been used successfully in seminaries. The critical response of other students as well as that of the instructor enhances the students' own reflection on practice.

Similarly, seminary faculties in pastoral counseling have devised effective methods for engendering reflection on practice in hospitals. Qualified and experienced supervisors are able to strengthen the students' abilities in pastoral visitation and counseling. The students also are able to learn about group dynamics and to improve their own style of relating to other people.

One other possibility at the seminary for experience in reflective practice is the worship of the seminary community itself. The theological school is not a church, and its worship is not the same as worship in a local congregation. But the worship in the seminary is not simulation, either. It is authentic worship in a Christian community, and as such it should be sensitive to both the historical liturgies and the contemporary issues of Christian practice. It would, therefore, be useful for students to be able to reflect on their worship experience at the seminary with a view toward improving their understanding of leadership in worshiping congregations.

The seminary is not and never has been adequately equipped to develop skills in reflective practice for all the functions of ministry. This is partly due to the short time span of seminary education, but the primary reason lies in the fact that many functions cannot be practiced away from the churches. Recognition of these limitations will enable both the seminaries and the churches to plan more effectively for their cooperative venture in the education of practical theologians.

C. Practical Christian Thinking About the Profession

We have argued that the practical theologian's primary work is to guide the church in its reflection on appropriate practice for authentic Christian living. Moreover, we have said that authentic Christian practice is, to a great extent, specific to one's vocation. Thus, not only is practical Christian thinking about the great issues facing humanity necessary for the Christian community; it is also important that individual Christians think about their practice of a specific vocation. It is here that the reflective practice and the practical Christian thinking required of the pastor come together. *What* the pastors are to do must always be decided according to their understanding of who they are as Christians. Therefore, the selection of priorities with respect to functions or duties requires practical Christian thinking. Moreover, the functional style of a reflective practitioner grows out of thinking about what it means to be a Christian relating to a congregation as a leader.

Some of this sort of thinking does and should go on *in* reflective practice, but it is so important to the practical theologian who is also a pastor that we believe that reflection *on* the practice of pastoral ministry in general is required as part of the curriculum.

It is possible, of course, to do practical Christian thinking in relation to courses that provide instruction on the nature of the congregation and the functional skills of practice. In fact, none of these courses will be appropriate for professional pastors unless there is a critical appraisal of institutional life and functional models for skills from the perspective of Christian identity. That has already been made abundantly clear. But more than this is needed. At some point, the seminary must provide an opportunity for practical theologians to engage in disciplined dialogue and reflection about the nature of the profession and its context as such.

There is a significant set of questions which might be probed in depth. For example:

1. What is ministry and how is it related to ordained ministry?

2. How should a pastor order priorities and which of the expected functions of ministry should have priority and on what grounds?

3. What is the authority of ministry and how is that authority to be exercised in structured power relationships?

This list is, of course, merely suggestive, but it does indicate a range of inquiry that is essential but not specifically attended to in other parts of the curriculum of most theological schools. We, therefore, recommend that a course be included in the curriculum which will address itself specifically to practical Christian thinking about the pastoral ministry. The point of the course would not be to draw final conclusions about the nature of pastoral leadership, but to encourage students to develop a habit of practical thinking about what they are doing, where they are doing it, and how they will go about it *as Christians.*

This sort of reflection must also continue during the probationary period. The education which will take place in the churches will, of course, emphasize the sorts of experiences that will enhance the ability of the probationary ordinands to perform the functions of the pastoral ministry effectively. Yet the seminary and the church together must insure that at no point do the ordinands lose sight of the fact that all of the functions of pastoral ministry are grounded in Christian identity and practical Christian thinking about the ministry and the congregational context of ministry.

Hopefully, this will stimulate an ongoing process of reflection as the students shape their ministries in new contexts. Such thinking creates the possibility for a synthesis of practical Christian thought and reflective practice. Assisting students in the forging of that synthesis is the most important contribution the seminary and the churches can make to the education of practical theologians.

In summary, we have argued that the education of practical theologians is the joint task of the church and the seminary. While the church must assume a major responsibility for education for pastoral reflection in practice, the seminary makes its major contribution by providing opportunities for reflection *on* the practice of Christian leaders in general and specifically on the practice of pastors. The outcome of such a partnership could be the emergence of a new generation of practical theologians sensitive to the nature of the churches' institutions and prepared to challenge them with a new vision for their future.

Conclusion

The proposals we have made would involve real change in the content and style of seminary education. But they are not "radical." We could have proposed changes that would in many ways seem more exciting. For example, we have assumed a system of courses much like those that now exist. Indeed, our proposals would tend to lead to rather tightly prescribed curricula. We could have recommended instead that the students be treated on a thoroughly personal basis and guided through the learning process by tutors at their own pace and according to the sequence of study that fits their individual needs. But we do not know of any seminaries with the capabilities of implementing such a program well.

We have assumed also existing faculties with their disciplinary commitments. We have asked them only not to impose the disciplinary style upon seminary students. We would prefer communities of free spiritis who in their own thinking and research were not the products of the established patterns of graduate education.

We have assumed that faculties will retain their privileges and their middle-class North American style of life. While we study the implications of the global situation for Christian life and action, we will continue to live in ways that are quite inappropriate to it. We could dream of communities so dedicated that as seminaries they would model the sharing and frugality to which we think we are called, using surplus resources in ways that genuinely empower the poor.

We could go on, but that is not our task. We are interested in making proposals that most seminary faculties in North America can seriously consider. We will rejoice if others draw from our analysis more radical conclusions for Christian discipleship, and experiment with truly new ways of preparing pastors for ministry in today's world. But perhaps the steps we do propose are needed before most of us, teachers, students, staff, and administrators, will be ready to think about radical discipleship or will have constituencies that would support it.

We offer now a specific curricular proposal. We do not expect anyone to follow it in detail. We are not sure that as we approached implementation we would do so ourselves. Nevertheless, it has seemed to us that the more specific we are the better. It is well to see what theoretical proposals might mean in practice. Hence, we conclude this chapter with a list of courses that could constitute the type of curriculum we have advocated. Such a list will make clear what is omitted as well as what is included.

The proposal assumes a curriculum of six semesters with four courses in each semester plus one summer of clinical training. We would be pleased to propose a four year program, or one based on extensive prerequisites. But we wanted to show that our recommendations can be implemented within the most limited realistic time frame of education for pastoral ministry.

A CURRICULUM

I. *The Heritage That Shapes Our Identity*   *7 Courses*

    A. *The origins of our faith through the Babylonian Exile.*
(Attention should be given to the contributions of near-Eastern peoples to the shaping of Jewish faith.)

    B. *Post-exilic Judaism through the final Jewish Revolt.*
(Attention should be given to Greek influences on Jewish faith.)

    C. *The New Testament and the Origins of Christian Faith.* (2 courses)
(Attention should be given to the Jewish context as well as Greek and Roman sources.)

    D. *Christianity and Judaism through the 16th Century.*
(Attention should be given to both Eastern and Western Christianity, and a clear focus should be included on key developments in liturgy and doctrine. The course should include some sections on key thinkers such as Augustine, Thomas, Luther, and Calvin. The thought of Plato and Aristotle as they were appropriated by Christians, Jews, and Muslims should be explained. Along with particular attention to the Reformation and the Counter-Reformation, some study of the rise of Islam and its relation to Christianity and the development of the Rabbinic traditions should be included.)

    E. *Christianity and Judaism from the 17th Century to the Present.*
(Attention should be given to developments in Orthodoxy, Roman Catholicism, Protestantism, and Judaism and their relationship to each other. Some discussion of the Enlightenment and its consequences should be included. The development of the missionary movement, the rise and fall of colonialism, and the emergence of indigenous churches should be part of the course of study. Of particular interest would be the Protestant ecumenical movement, the impact of the Holocaust, and the beginning of interreligious dialogue. Major theologians such as Schleiermacher, Kierkegaard, Barth, and Bultmann should be discussed along with the rise of historical criticism and its general impact on biblical studies. Also the thought and influence of other major thinkers, such as Descartes, Hume, Kant, Hegel, and Marx should be treated.)

    F. *North American Religious History from the Colonial Period to the Present.*
(Here special attention should be given to denomination history with students being given time to study their own denominations in some detail. Careful attention should be given to the emergence of black Christianity and other ethnic contributions to the church. The rise of the feminist theological movement should be noted and at least one major feminist theologian and one major black theologian should be examined along with white male representatives.)

II.   *The Global Context of Our Lives*   *1 Course*

(An analysis of world hunger and oppression showing the interconnection of economic and political forces with ecological decay, population growth, racism, and sexism. An analysis of present American culture and economy and its impact on the globe. Some discussion of the role of the churches, both actual and potential, should be included.)

III. *Issues for Practical Christian Thinking*   *7 Courses*

Required Courses:
A. How can we make sense of our doctrinal heritage in our post-Enlightenment age?
B. What does the reality of Buddhism (or Hinduism or Islam) say to us about our faith and our mission?

Five Elective Courses:
A. What is the church's mission today?
B. How are we to understand our sexuality and our gender differences?
C. What does Liberation Theology say to the North American churches?
D. What is the Christian response to world hunger or the nuclear arms race?
E. How does the church rightly relate to the political order?
F. What are the responsibilities of the church in the age of electronic media?
G. What is an appropriate form of Christian sprituality today?

IV.   *Professional Preparation for Pastoral Ministry*   *9 Courses +*
                                                      1 Summer Internship

A. *Reflection on Models of Practice.* (2 courses)
   Models for Pastoral Counselors, Religious Educators, and Church Managers. (Much of the reflection to be on the sociological, psychological, and theological foundations.)
B. *Reflection on the Congregational Context of Pastoral Ministry.* (1 course)
C. *Opportunities for Reflective Practice.* (5 course equivalent)
   1. Preaching and Worship. (3 courses)
       (Attention should be given to the use of media.)
   2. Clinical Pastoral Education. (summer 2 course equivalent)
D. *Contextual Education.* (2 course equivalent)
   (The contextual component may be attached to any of the courses in sections A and B above.)
E. *Practical Christian Thinking about Pastoral Ministry.* (1 course)

In conclusion, we would point out once again that this book has been an example of doing practical theology. We have faced a practical problem in the life of the church: how best to educate its leaders. We have tried to understand that problem in terms of its history, the present condition of the seminaries we know best, and relevant cultural considerations. We have sought the solution to the problem *as Christians* in terms of our Christian memory and our understanding of its implications. And we have done all of this while reflecting on our own practice as theological educators.

We mention this again not to ask that others model their practical Christian thinking on ours, but to make it clear that such thinking can and does occur. It can be learned. We believe that the renewal of the church depends on many Christians becoming practical Christian thinkers even while engaging in reflective practice of their own. In other words, we are persuaded that all Christian leaders should become practical theologians who ground their daily decisions in practical Christian thinking.

Author Index